# LAUGHOLOGY

## IMPROVE YOUR LIFE WITH

## THE SCIENCE OF LAUGHTER

## STEPHANIE DAVIES

Crown House Publishing Limited
www.crownhouse.co.uk
www.crownhousepublishing.com

First published by
Crown House Publishing Ltd
Crown Buildings, Bancyfelin, Carmarthen, Wales, SA33 5ND, UK
**www.crownhouse.co.uk**

and

Crown House Publishing Company LLC
PO Box 2223, Williston, VT 05495, USA
**www.crownhousepublishing.com**

First printed 2013. Reprinted 2014, 2015, 2016, 2017, 2018.

Cover image and page 70 © Interfoto/Alamy
Images page 15, 42 and 115 © sabri deniz kizil - Fotolia.com
Image page 41 © Alfonso de Tomás - Fotolia.com
Image page 50 © abeadev - Fotolia.com
Image page 67 © olly - Fotolia.com

British Library Cataloguing-in-Publication Data
A catalogue entry for this book is available from the British Library.

Print ISBN 978-184590792-1
Mobi ISBN 978-184590811-9
ePub ISBN 978-184590812-6

LCCN 2011940613

Printed and bound in the UK by
TJ International, Padstow, Cornwall

To all the people I have had the privilege of working with and helping over the years – you have all helped me as much as I have hopefully helped you. To the wonderful children, young people and carers at Claire House Hospice in Merseyside who continue to inspire me every day. But most of all this is to my family who are all brilliant and funny.

# ACKNOWLEDGEMENTS

I would like to thank all the services that have believed in and used the Laughology model through the years and who continue to use it to improve lives and potential.

I would also like to thank Caroline Lenton who believed in *Laughology*, the book, and the team at Crown House for giving me the opportunity to write it.

My mum who has been a supporter and promoter of Laughology from the beginning. My dad, who always has made me laugh and encouraged me to believe I can be and do anything. My step-mum Marian, Aunt Michele, Susie, Paul and cousin Alex who tirelessly drove me to gigs and events and listened to my comedy material before it was funny, but supported me and clapped as if it was. My brother Daniel and sisters Ruth, Fiona and Beth and step-brother Paul who all make me laugh and have believed in me from the very beginning and have supported me through the triumphs and tribulations of running a business which hasn't seemed so funny at times. All my nieces and nephews who continue to remind me of the importance of having a young outlook, playing and having fun: Ryan, Jade, Jack, Ben, Max, Holly and Thomas. My wonderful partner Nick Harding who has been the main ingredient for my happiness and who took the time to cast his experienced eye over my humble writings, and Millie and Lucas who sat patiently and played while he did.

To all my wonderful friends, I cannot name them all, but each is important and has supported me and constantly asked, 'So when is the book out again?', making sure I did actually finish it.

And a huge thank you to the brilliant Laughology team, Kerry Leigh, Juliette Yardley, Alan Matthews, David Keeling and Maurice De Castro, who continue to promote and build Laughology and without whom I wouldn't have been able to spend time writing this book.

Thank you all.

# CONTENTS

# PROLOGUE

## LAUGHOLOGY: A WORKBOOK FOR A NEW MODEL OF LIVING

At the height of laughter, the universe is flung into a kaleidoscope of new possibilities.

Jean Houston

At 14 I was lucky enough to get the chance to work with one of the greatest comics of the 21st century: the late Norman Wisdom. Norman professed to have had an unhappy childhood. 'All my boyhood all I ever wanted was to be loved', he told me. In later life, not only did Norman use humour and laughter to entertain, he also used them as a way to help himself through difficult times. One day on set we were talking about his childhood and I mentioned some difficulties I was going through, as teenagers do. Norman's words seemed to make more sense to me than any advice I had been given before: 'Stephanie, laughter truly is the best medicine; if you can laugh and make others laugh you'll always get by.'

I remember thinking he was right; it was simple, laughter really does lift your spirits. I love laughing; I don't know anyone who doesn't (unless you have asthma, in which case laughter isn't always the best medicine – Ventolin is). It was at this point that I decided I wanted to make people laugh too, much to the disappointment of my teachers. I started to become more aware of my own sense of humour and how laughter made me feel, how I used it and how others used it – family, friends and people on TV. I learnt my humour skills from a variety of places, mainly my dad who was always a joker and managed to create laughter even in the most difficult circumstances. I quickly learned to use laughter as a coping mechanism for the ups and downs of adolescence. My school report read: 'Stephanie is always the class joker and does well when she has centre stage, though she needs to learn that joking and clowning around is not a career option.'

During my final year of university I started writing and performing comedy. After being offered an open mic spot at a local comedy club, I realised I had found my forte and became a working comedian – making a living 'joking and clowning around'.

While learning my stage-craft, the words of Norman Wisdom resonated in mind. I realised he was right: laughter and humour are the key to getting by in life. Not only were they providing me with earnings, they were helping me to see life clearly, gain perspective and become a more resilient, confident and happier human being. There is no other place you need to be more resilient than as a woman in a comedy club on a Friday or Saturday night.

As my career as a comedian took off, my sense of humour developed further and I looked to my own life and the world around me for observations I could use to twist and turn into comedy routines. The more I did this the more I found my perspective on life changed, and more often than not a problem would become potential for a routine. Once I had flipped the situation on its head and found the 'humour perspective' I would feel better about the issue, and when I felt better it would be easier for me to move forward and solve the problem.

So that is what this book is about: the choices we make that enable us to see life in different ways and the tools and techniques that allow us to do this.

In the past 12 years my comedy career has evolved into a vocation, which is still based in laughter and humour but is now more person-focused. My passion remains laughter and humour but now that passion goes deeper than standing on a stage and hoping people find me funny. Nowadays my work is about helping others to be happy, to achieve more and to think, feel and work better.

Since starting a career in the laughter business in 2001, I've been developing ways to help others use laughter and humour as a personal development tool – I call this technique Laughology. It has been built on my understanding of humour and laughter as a comedian and also from a psychology point of view. More recently I have been lucky enough to study for an MA at the University of Chester, making links between humour, laughter, psychology and health, while also practising these techniques in specialist mental health units.

I have been fortunate to work in a variety of settings with individuals and groups with mild to moderate and acute mental health issues. Laughology has been delivered successfully in small and large organisations to encourage thinking skills, positive engagement, organisational development and great leadership, as well as to enhance health and well-being in many different settings – from schools and hospitals to some of the top blue-chip companies in the world.

Some of the greatest comedians have lived with disorders including depression and bipolar. It seems that if you peer behind the laughter and smiles you will sometimes find someone who has faced many challenges in life. Humour, laughter and comedy can be a way to cope with these challenges: they are survival tools that we can all tap into.

It is an ancient truism that 'laughter is the best medicine' and for aeons humans have enjoyed a good giggle. The pleasure and joy that a good laugh can bring to individuals and groups is of immeasurable worth, although it can be dismissed too easily as simplistic or not sufficiently scientific to be considered as a tool for coping. Not only is humour quite rightly regarded as a positive emotion – a pleasant thing to share with friends and something you look for in a partner (must have a GSOH) – but its outward manifestation, laughter, is a universal currency. No matter where in the world you are, the slightest hint of a smile can immediately connect strangers, no matter what the language and cultural barriers may be.

Although we are all born with the capacity to process humorous circumstances, it is also a skill that can be improved and honed. We develop and evolve this ability throughout our lives – influenced by family, peers and experience – learning when and how to use it. But can humour be controlled? Can we consciously harness this innate ability and use it whenever we want to improve our communication and relationships, enhance our well-being and bring joy to others?

The simple answer is yes – and, using the techniques developed by Laughology, this practical guide is going to show you how.

Laughology is about understanding how we process information from the outside world and then respond and react to these circumstances internally. It uses a flexible cognitive approach that is easy to learn, sustainable and adaptable to many situations. Laughology fundamentals are based in science and psychology but it is not rocket science. While, over the following pages, I will be explaining how humour and laughter affect us on a behavioural and biological level, you don't need be a doctor or a psychologist to understand Laughology. It is simple and practical. You may even judge that many of the techniques I outline are common sense. You'd be right – they are. However, humour and laughter are often sadly neglected in many people's lives. If something happens that makes us laugh we enjoy it but, as a rule, few of us are proactive when it comes to finding ways to introduce more laughter and humour into our lives. We might make sure we find time in our busy schedule to spend an hour at the gym every few days (for the record, that is a very good thing to do too), but how many of us take a few minutes each day to think about how we are going to laugh more, be happy and what makes us happy?

But Laughology is much more than just showing you ways to be happier. It provides you with a means to use humour and laughter to enhance thinking skills on every level for positive well-being, resilience and communication. To explain this further we need to think about how laughter and humour can fit into our emotional processing. As we absorb information from our external environment our emotions are affected. This, in turn, dictates our language and behaviour. The way we act and the things we say subsequently influence other's reactions towards us, which again feeds into the way in which we subsequently behave.

Typically what happens is that an external event is processed through our internal mental mechanisms and we make an *internal representation* (IR) of that event. The IR, combined with the corresponding physiological response, creates a *state*. State is the internal emotional condition of an individual – happy, sad, motivated and so on.

An individual's IR of a situation can be distorted by previous experience and by how we feel at that time, the other people involved and our personal history. These may cause us to interpret an event either negatively or positively. Our IR of any given situation will include pictures, sounds, dialogue and emotions; for example, whether we feel motivated, challenged, pleased or excited. A given state is the result of the combination of our IR and physiological reactions. Recognising that we communicate, perform and react better in a positive state, where we can engage our rational mind and perspective, enables us to develop a more affirmative methodology for controlling that state. This means we are in a stronger position to obtain the results we desire. Humour can be used as a way to process and change the IR of a situation, therefore gaining a different perspective and state.

This way of processing information is easy to see in some of the greatest comedians, some of whom have used their challenging life stories to provide comic material. They change their IR. Billy Connolly is a great practitioner of this technique. After surviving a difficult childhood of physical and mental abuse he rose to fame as a comedian, often using reinterpreted recollections of his past to entertain audiences.

Laughology is the study of this psychology and offers strategies for feeling better and enhancing living based on what humans do naturally as a coping mechanism. The model uses humour and laughter to encourage perspective in order to gain control over our emotions so we can move forward effectively, with better results and greater happiness.

# HOW TO USE THIS BOOK

Laughology is a tool to help you improve your life in every way, so this book has been written as a practical guide with exercises for you to do throughout. Use this book, write in it, underline bits you like, add your own notes in the work pages at the back and record your own thoughts.

The concepts and exercises presented in this book are particularly for those who want an alternative attitude and way of thinking for improving life and work. The benefits of using humour as a system for processing information will be shown in a practical and descriptive way. Do try to complete the exercises in each chapter – this will help you to use the Laughology model, personalise the experience and think realistically about how you can apply Laughology in your life. Along the way there will be case studies (with names changed to protect identities). You will learn how real people have used Laughology, what worked for them and how you can benefit. If you follow the simple guidelines they'll work for you too. Remember: this is a new way of thinking so you will have to practise and work at it. Like anything, the more you put in, the more you'll get out of it. Each chapter also includes a summary of the key learning points.

Laughology is also based on my personal successes in improving the life and work of clients from many different backgrounds. Laughology has been used by thousands of people nationally and internationally in a variety of different settings: in blue-chip companies to boost staff morale and productivity, in retail businesses to improve customer service and in rehabilitation programmes to enhance recovery. It has also been used by public health bodies to help people with a range of mild to more severe mental health issues.

There's a reason why Laughology has been and is so successful: it works, it's simple, it makes you feel better and anyone can do it. More importantly, it's sustainable because humour and laughter are coping skills that we all possess and have the ability to develop. This book is a simple guide to help you do this.

# SIGNS AND SYMBOLS

This book has been written so it can be used as a practical guide; therefore I want to make it as easy as possible for you to use, dip in and out of, write in and refer to whenever and wherever you like.

The book follows a basic pattern with Part One structured in the following way:

 *Story* relating to the topic.

 Explanation of what we are talking about – a general understanding of the topic in *context*.

 The *science* – a scientific explanation of the topic using popular psychology such as cognitive-behavioural therapy and recent research to support why the theory and application work.

 *Practical application* – each chapter has practical exercises to go with the topic. These will help you understand more deeply how this can relate to you and your life.

 *Points to remember* – at the end of each chapter you'll find a short summary of the important things to remember.

---

 In Part Two I describe the Humour Toolkit, FLIP (Focus, Language, Imagination, Pattern breaking), which will give you the ability to improve the way you look at life by building cognitive skills. These chapters are laid out differently and focus on how to use FLIP in everyday life.

---

 In Part Three I outline the five steps of SMILE (Smile, Moment of magic, Impulse, Laughter, Empower); a simple process to finding positives in your life. This chapter is more practical and also differs from the guides in Part One.

# PART ONE

## STORY, CONTEXT, SCIENCE, PRACTICAL APPLICATION, POINTS TO REMEMBER

# CHAPTER 1

# WHAT IS LAUGHTER?

 ## A TIME AND A *PLAICE* FOR LAUGHTER

While visiting a secure mental health hospital in West Virginia with Dr Hunter 'Patch' Adams and his team it struck me just how powerful laughter can be in helping to build relationships and communication with others.[1] I had teamed up with some fabulous people from the Gesundheit! Institute and we had been to various centres and hospitals around the region using laughter and humour to help bring joy to a diverse range of patients.

As we were leaving the final hospital there was a room no one had entered. I peeked in and noticed a man, perhaps in his mid-forties, in a chair, rocking back and forth, making a noise and in a state with which I was unfamiliar. It was at this point that I questioned what I was doing. Was taking laughter into places like this beneficial or was I way out of my depth? I had never encountered a situation like this before and

---

1   In 2006 I was lucky enough to win a scholarship to join Patch Adams and his team at a training centre in West Virginia. Patch is one of the pioneers of humour and laughter in health care and has worked tirelessly over the past 30-plus years to promote peace, happiness and justice around the world. A film, *Patch Adams* (starring Robin Williams as Patch), was released in 1998 and helped to promote Patch's vision and story. It publicised the work of the world famous Gesundheit! Institute, a hospital and wellness centre where humour, happiness, creativity and positivity are as important as medical knowledge and scientific practice.

wondered whether to walk on, as most of the others had done, or to test my understanding of the power of laughter and step into the room.

Armed with nothing but my sense of fun and a plastic fish I decided this was it: I had to go in to either prove or disprove everything I had believed in up to this point. Could this individual's life be improved with laughter, humour and a smile? Could I reach out to this person with something so simplistic when he seemed so far removed from this world? I was unsure how I would even start.

I entered the room and bent down by his side, smiling, trying to catch his eye, using the prop and the last ounce of energy I had. As he looked at me I could see that there was a way I could connect with him, so I did everything in my power to make him laugh. I waved my plastic fish, made some silly noises and told some funny stories about my day. All of a sudden the man let out a huge guffaw. I don't know whether he was laughing at me or with me (perhaps he was thinking 'it should be you in here!'), but whatever it was, we connected; we connected on a level that was wonderfully friendly, happy and equal. His laughter only lasted about ten seconds but afterwards his whole face had lifted and he made eye contact with me until we said our goodbyes.

At that moment it was confirmed to me that laughter is a powerful communication tool that can be used with anyone anywhere. Laughter knows no boundaries when it comes to age, race or gender. A laugh or a smile in Iceland is the same as a laugh or a smile in India or England – what a great level of communication to get by on!

 # THE FEEL-GOOD FACTOR

We have all been supplied with the ability to laugh. Research suggests that it is innate because, as Donald Brown points out in his book *Human Universals*, laughter is found in every society – even children who are deaf and blind, and can't see or hear other people laughing, still laugh.[2] Robert Provine, in his book *Laughter: A Scientific Investigation*, puts forward the theory that laughter is a form of com-

---

2    D. Brown, *Human Universals* (New York: McGraw-Hill, 1991).

munication, probably the first one in the human race, which later evolved, with the emancipation of the voice, into language.[3]

Research into why we laugh and where it comes from is still in its infancy, but what we do know is that it feels good. Laughter is a natural tonic and can have positive bodily effects. Biologically it produces happy hormones, known as endorphins, which help to create positive emotions and can change the chemical make-up in the brain to produce serotonin. As well as these chemical effects, laughter can give us a break from what we are thinking about or doing, especially when these are stressful or upsetting. How often have you been in a situation where you are highly stressed or anxious and something is said or done that makes you laugh, and all of a sudden you feel better or more comfortable about the situation and the people you are with?

Laughter helps us move forward, it empowers us and makes us feel better. So by understanding more about where, how and what encourages laughter, we can start to understand what behaviours, thoughts and situations promote more laughter. Therefore helping with a more rational way of thinking and behaving, resulting in a happier approach to life. Activities that cause stress can leave us stuck in situations or lead to recurring patterns in life and relationships which generate negative emotions, thoughts and behaviours, so understanding a strategy to move forward, using thinking techniques can be helpful.

 ## SO, LAUGHTER ...?

Laughter is about relationships, it's not about jokes. It's a form of communication.

Robert R. Provine

The *Oxford English Dictionary* definition of laughter is 'to make the spontaneous sounds and movements of the face and body that are the instinctive expressions of lively amusement and sometimes also of derision'. Laughter can be an audible expression, often perceived as the appearance of merriment or amusement. We can laugh to ourselves about an inner thought or laughter may follow as a physiological

3   R. R. Provine, *Laughter: A Scientific Investigation* (New York: Viking Books, 2000).

reaction from external stimuli – a song or joke, tickling and many other things.

So, we know laughter is part of human behaviour and works with the body and brain. It can help to clarify meanings in a social situation and provides an emotional context to conversations. It can be used as a signal for being part of a group – indicating acceptance and positive interactions with others. The physical expression of laughter is the same in all of us and was described anatomically by Charles Darwin in 1872.[4] In other words, if nothing else, from early on we all understand the same *ha ha*; it seems to be both instinctive and primitive, even prior to the development of language itself. Laughter really is a communicative tool; it conveys how we feel about situations to the outside world. It is important to recognise here that laughter isn't always about feeling upbeat and happy. Sometimes it can be induced by nerves, embarrassment and even shock. Ultimately, it is an outward indication of how we want to communicate to others how we feel, or at least how we want them to perceive how we feel.

Laughter can be contagious, as the chuckling of one person can itself provoke amusement in other people. It has been known for some time that we often mirror behaviours when talking to others, mimicking gestures and even tone and pitch. Tests at Imperial College and University College London (UCL) found that laughter causes us to do the same and triggers a behavioural response in the brain.[5] According to scientists, this reaction occurs in a brain area that is activated when we smile. 'It seems that it's absolutely true that "laugh and the whole world laughs with you",' says Dr Sophie Scott from the Institute of Cognitive Neuroscience at UCL.[6]

The theory of just how contagious laughter can be was put to the test by the researchers using a group of human guinea pigs; they were wired up to MRI scanners which allowed the scientists to monitor

---

4   C. Darwin, *The Expressions of Emotions in Man and Animals*, 1st edn (London: John Murray, 1872).

5   J. E. Warren, D. A. Sauter, F. Eisner, J. Wiland, M. A. Dresner, J. S. Wise, S. Rosen and S. K. Scott, 'Positive emotions preferentially engage an auditory–motor "mirror" system', *Journal of Neuroscience* 26 (2006), 13067–13075.

6   Wellcome Trust, 'Laugh and the whole world laughs with you: why the brain just can't help itself' (13 December 2006). Press release available at http://www.wellcome. ac.uk/News/Media-office/Press-releases/2006/WTX034939.htm/ (accessed 31 May 2012).

what was happening deep in their brains. Some of the test subjects were lucky and listened to the sound of human laughter; others were subjected to unpleasant sounds which included screams and barfing (that's retching to those who prefer an academic description). Every sound elicited a response in the premotor cortical region – an area which prepares muscles in the face to communicate an expression in reaction to the sound. However, the response was greater for positive sounds, suggesting that laughter is indeed contagious.

Laughter is really contagious; the brain primes us to laugh and smile by mirroring the behaviour of others, this helps us to interact socially.

The researchers believe this explains why we respond to laughter or cheering with an involuntary smile. 'We usually encounter positive emotions, such as laughter or cheering, in group situations, whether watching a comedy programme with family or a football game with friends,' said Scott. 'This response in the brain, automatically priming us to smile or laugh, provides a way of mirroring the behaviour of others, something which helps us interact socially. It could play an important role in building strong bonds between individuals in a group.'

Laughter is a multifaceted communicative tool that has taken millions of years to evolve. We still do not completely understand how it developed and we are only just starting to understand why we have it and how we use it. We'll look at this in more depth in later chapters. Now it's your turn to understand your own laughter.

# LAUGHTER AND YOU

By exploring what we think laughter is and understanding how it can be used, we can start to see the power behind this simple tool for feeling better. And when we feel better we communicate more effectively, enabling us to be proactive and work through feelings rather than reacting and responding with a behaviour that can lead to negative outcomes.

Write down what you believe laughter is – good and bad:

.......................................................................

.......................................................................

.......................................................................

Now think about how many times a day you laugh. When it's 'good' laughter, what types of things cause this laughter?

Think about where you use laughter and how you use it. Who do you laugh with the most? When do you laugh the most? Write down as much information about what triggers your good laughter below:

.......................................................................

.......................................................................

.......................................................................

By understanding what we in Laughology call your 'laughter triggers' – the thoughts and feelings which get you into a state where laughter is more likely to happen – you can start to recognise how you can consciously bring on this state and what behaviours are more conducive to you feeling upbeat and positive. Identifying these triggers is an important part of understanding what motivates us to feel better.

# POINTS TO REMEMBER

- Laughter is innate – we are born with the ability to laugh.
- Laughter is not always about the happy things in life; it's natural to laugh at shocking and sometimes sad things.
- We can learn to laugh more.
- Laughter is contagious.

## CHAPTER 2

# YOUR LAUGHTER TRIGGERS

 ## TOILET HUMOUR

Children and the things they say often make me laugh because of their innocent understanding of the world and the way they communicate this to one another and to grown-ups. Children have a great sense of humour; they don't care as much as adults about what they say or what others think about them when they dance on their own, skip in the street, talk to themselves or noisily state their views. This is something you learn as you grow up and try to conform to society's rules. Granted, this childlike view of the world can get them into trouble at times, but it's a lovely quality too. As we get older it is necessary to learn social boundaries, although we usually start worrying too much about what people might think of us if we do/say something unusual. We lose our sense of humour when we make mistakes and see these expressions of ourselves as embarrassing or uncomfortable.

I was in a large superstore with my sister and her daughter when my niece said, in a very loud voice, that she needed to go to the toilet. So off we went to the ladies. I went into one cubicle and my sister and niece went into the one next to me. All of a sudden I heard my niece say, 'Mummy, are you having a poo?' There was a brief silence and then my sister said, louder than was necessary, 'No, Jade, of course I'm not. Don't be so silly.' Without missing a beat – the timing couldn't have been better – my niece replied, 'Yes you are mummy, I can smell it!' My poor sister emerged from the toilet rather red-faced to confront a queue of very amused women, only some of whom were polite enough to pretend, in a very British way, that they had heard none of what had just occurred, while the others, including myself, laughed out loud – and by way of compensation gave her a sympathetic look.

To this day, when I recall that story I can feel the laughter bubbling inside me as if I could really laugh out loud again. Just imagining the situation makes me smile and I can see clearly my sister's flushed face as she emerged from the cubicle. It's one of my many laughter triggers that can instantly bring on a positive feeling. Not necessarily laugh out loud, but it does help to lift my mood. I have many other laughter triggers and have written some down which helps me to remember them.

 # LAUGHTER BRAIN-TRAINING

Knowing what triggers your laughter is important. These are the thoughts or memories that take us to a place in time that was enjoyable, fun and made us laugh or smile. We all have these recollections. Sometimes we think of them and find ourselves laughing. Simply by recalling that thought, our emotional response to the memory is triggered and our mood is changed. Thoughts affect mood and mood affects thought; when we become aware of this we can take more control of how we respond to our thoughts and feelings. Recognising that we can work through a thought or feeling to figure out the best response, rather than simply reacting to the feeling, can help to enhance relationships and communication on every level.

Reactions of this sort can happen with sad and negative memories too. But we can train our brain to override negative thoughts and replace them with positive ones that make us feel better. The more you do this the better you get at doing it, until eventually it will be automatic and you will be able to lift your mood and think in a more affirmative way almost subconsciously.

We can bring these positive triggers into our mind at those times when we feel down to take our mind off unpleasant thoughts and feelings. A list of positive triggers can be used for this purpose.

 # TURNING A NEGATIVE INTO A POSITIVE

Our thoughts have a profound effect on our emotions. By learning how to think more optimistically, we improve our emotional state and can take better charge of our emotions, rather than allowing them to take charge of us in a negative way.

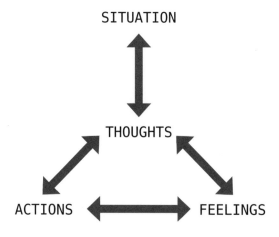

We may not realise it but our thoughts also affect our feelings. Some people think it is the other way round, but the more we become aware of the interplay between thoughts and feelings, the more we recognise how they influence each other. For example, when you have negative thoughts (it could be about work or a relationship) they have a habit of making you feel anxious or gloomy; you become upset and down in the dumps. By having a stock of good thoughts – your laughter triggers – you can instantly distract the negative thought pattern. This can take seconds and it can be very discreet. Once you feel better emotionally, you can think more logically and productively. You can start to put negative thoughts into perspective by asking yourself questions like: What can I do to make this situation better? Does the negative thought represent what is actually happening or going to happen in reality? If not, how can I produce a more positive outcome with a positive thought?

Negative thoughts and feelings can take hold of us, so it's important to recognise them first as negative thoughts and start the process every time we have one, replacing it with a good thought by utilising our laughter triggers.

Fears can stem from exaggerated negative thoughts. I think very visually and often this can impact on my fear of spiders. I understand the irrational thought patterns I have relating to them but this doesn't stop the fear. When I see a spider the immediate thought I have is that it is going to hurt me. I also have an image in my head of the spider jumping or crawling on me.

There is a two-pronged technique to deal with irrational thoughts like these:

1    Identify the thoughts as irrational and negative. This awareness is the first step to being able to deal with them in a positive way as you are recognising that they are habitual and can be changed.

2    Interrupt the thought using humour and your laughter triggers. This breaks the thought pattern and diverts your thinking. This allows you to make a better decision based on the reality of the situation and not an exaggerated version you may have visualised.

I deal with spiders by giving them a comedy name like Sybil or Cyril. I often visualise them wearing little shoes and busying themselves with daily tasks like humans do. Doing this contains the fear as it distracts my negative thought process and produces a different thought response in my brain. I no longer respond to the spider as a threat but see it for what it is: a small creature that is scared of me. This takes time, effort and focused thinking, but it does generate results.

The human brain is complex. It produces plenty of rational thoughts which allow us to make successful decisions in life, but it also produces irrational thoughts. It is common for someone with irrational and negative thoughts to give meaning to them and believe they are true.

This isn't always appropriate. Humour can take the power out of the meaning and support a more positive response.

# WHAT MAKES YOU FEEL GOOD?

Laughology is about using positive situations and triggers to make it easier to feel good about ourselves and help others. Think of as many laughter triggers as you can – take your time and think through each one separately before you write them down. They can be anything from a time when you felt really happy, like the memory of a wonderful holiday, a much-loved pet, a lovely time spent with family or friends, winning a prize, a celebratory cake, achieving something you set out to do or a favourite song or piece of music that really lifts your mood. A laughter trigger can be a joke, a TV comedy show, a funny film, a cartoon or comic book or your favourite comedian. Have you noticed that as you think of each item it brings a smile to your face? It's hard not to smile when we think of the things we like. It's perfectly natural. Your 'laughter muscles' can be exercised – and they grow. The more you laugh the bigger they get! Write down your laughter triggers here:

...................................................................................

...................................................................................

...................................................................................

Now look at your list. Which is your favourite? Can you put them in order? Which item is guaranteed to make you feel good or make you laugh out loud? Order them and choose your top five.

1    .......................................................................

2    .......................................................................

3    .......................................................................

4    .......................................................................

5    .......................................................................

These are your personal triggers. Keep them in your mind and use them whenever you need to lift your spirits. All you have to do is remember them and they will bring a smile to your face! Try to think of funny things every day: listen to what people say and observe events in daily life and family situations. It all has a comical angle if you look at it in the right way.

Sometimes when we feel sad, stressed or negative those feelings can overwhelm us and we get stuck in these thought patterns. List any negative thoughts you have regularly here:

.............................................................................

.............................................................................

.............................................................................

Once you've written the negative thought cross it out and replace it with a more positive one. A positive thought should be solution-focused and linked to a feeling, for example:

*Negative thought*: I can't ask for help with work as my boss will think I'm incapable and can't do my job.

*Positive thought*: If I ask for help, I will be able to move forward and complete the task quicker and feel better and less stressed.

By having positive triggers to hand, or as a list in your mind, you can take time – even if it's just one minute – to think about the trigger and break that negativity. Just distracting your mind from the negative situation or thought will help you feel better. When you feel better you behave and think better.

To take this one step further, can you turn your negative thought on its head? Is there a way you can take the power out of it by making it silly or humorous? Can you use a visualisation to do this or a colour that you could wash over the negative image if there is one? Remember anything is possible with humour as it's your imagination that enables it; cartoons are a great example of how humour can be used to make light of situations. Can you imagine someone, something or a situation in a more comical, cartoon-like way? The *Ally McBeal* series of the late 1990s used this method effectively. Maybe go online and watch a couple of clips to see how the main character used her humour and imagination to help her feel better in difficult situations.

Over the next week keep a diary of the times you thought about your triggers and write them down in your work pages. The more you use your laughter triggers the easier it gets. Pretty soon you'll be thinking more and more of the things that make you laugh and this will put a smile on your face and give you a lift. Ask others about their laughter triggers. Are they the same as yours?

Your overall happiness is dependent on your ability to manage negative thoughts. We all have them and it's pretty normal to get them stuck in your head. However, how you manage them is the key to moving forward and feeling better. The ratio of your negative to positive thoughts will determine how happy you are. Your brain is constantly monitoring the emotional tone of your thoughts – too many negative thoughts and your brain responds by creating stress and sadness in your body. When you add more positive thoughts your brain will create relaxation and happiness. By training yourself to deal with negative thoughts with more positive, logical and rational ones, you will improve your positive/negative thought ratio and feel happier. Using the techniques outlined above will help you do this.

The part of our brain that gives us the ability to think, the prefrontal cortex, is what makes the human brain so specialised and distinguishes us from other animals. By using our thoughts to refine and guide our emotions we are maximising our potential. While it's possible to change thoughts, it takes practice; like anything you want to get better at, you have to stick at it and practice, practice, practice.

List the top five positive thoughts you have about yourself that make you happy and can help you feel better in difficult situations. These should be amusing and comedic to help shift your mood and gain control of a difficult situation. The list will make it easier if you become stuck in negative thought patterns. These can be fun statements that take you back to a pleasurable time or place – for example: 'I am She-Ra, princess of power, and I have the power!' Or it might be a time you did something that made others laugh in a positive way; you may have even made yourself laugh.

1 ........................................................................

2 ........................................................................

3 ........................................................................

4 ........................................................................

5 ........................................................................

# POINTS TO REMEMBER

■ Start storing happy memories to feel better.

■ You can turn a negative into a positive.

■ Once you feel better emotionally you will think more constructively too.

# CHAPTER 3

# HAPPY PEOPLE

 ## GLASS HALF FULL

When Joe phoned me up out of the blue it is fair to say he was unhappy. So much so that his doctor had (unhelpfully) put him on antidepressants. Joe wasn't happy about being on pills and had discovered Laughology through an internet search. He was looking for someone or something that could help him feel more positive about his life and the situation in which he found himself.

At first I was apprehensive. It seemed to me that he was looking for a life coach, which I am not. However, he was adamant that from what he had seen on the Laughology website, the Laughology model could offer him real benefits and help him overcome the negativity of his situation. After a protracted discussion in which he explained the roots of his despair, I agreed to help.

Over the following month I met Joe regularly and began the process of unpicking and analysing the aspects of his life which had left him feeling so low. Joe hadn't always been unhappy. He was naturally inclined to be a glass half-full type of guy and part of the frustration he felt was because he couldn't understand how he had got himself in a rut.

Along with a partner Joe ran his own business which did very worthwhile community work. But times were hard and the company wasn't making much money. In order to set up the business Joe had sold his house to free up collateral and moved back in with his mother. On the face of it the root of Joe's unhappiness might appear obvious: he was struggling financially. But as I began to get to the underlying issues it became apparent that money wasn't a big driver in Joe's life.

He explained that the time in his life when he had been most happy was when he was working for a similar organisation to the one he now ran, but as a community worker rather than as a manager. He found real pleasure in helping people and making them happy. In his current position, as director of the company, his days were devoted to chasing money and not to the altruism that had previously attracted him to community work. He'd almost given up on the reason he started the business in the first place – to help people.

But this wasn't the only issue that was affecting him. It transpired that Joe felt he had been cajoled into starting the company by his partner – a friend who Joe admitted could be a bit forceful. Joe had been apprehensive about the business from the start but admitted that he felt overpowered into going into partnership with his co-director and that had left him feeling powerless. He explained that his partner was bullish and negative about many aspects of their working practices and that, because there was just the two of them, he felt isolated and alone at work. He reminisced about previous jobs where he had enjoyed the camaraderie of his colleagues.

There was also the issue of Joe's home life. To save money he had moved in with his mother and by his own admission he found this difficult. He described his mum as a negative influence.

The two main people in Joe's life – with whom he spent most time – were both having a harmful effect on the way he felt about his life and this was making him feel depressed. I surmised that money, or the lack of it, was a side concern. The real issue was these two relationships. His mum and business partner probably didn't even realise they were causing a problem, but the way Joe was responding to them was having a negative impact on the way he understood his life.

We all have people in our lives who we perceive as having a negative effect on us. In many cases it is not practical to just ignore them or cut ourselves off from them – they may be family members or work colleagues. Often we just grin and bear it: interact with them and walk away feeling infected by their negativity. What we often don't realise is that we *can* take control. It is not other people who make us unhappy per se; it is the way we react and respond to them. If you take responsibility for the impact people have on you, and change the way you behave towards them, then you will find that they will change the way they behave towards you. It may be uncomfortable at first, because you are setting new boundaries in a relationship, but ultimately you will feel empowered and in control – and that makes for happy individuals.

Joe and I mapped out the points in his life where he felt happiest and identified what made him happy. We then identified when and why this had changed and pinpointed what relationships in his life were making him feel unhappy. Next we worked out what he would need in order to shift from the unfulfilled state he was in to a more positive position. He needed to make big changes: he agreed that he would be happier if he gave up his business and also moved away from his mother.

He did both. He found a job in a different part of the country similar to the one he'd had done before he set up his own company and started a new life. He began working on community projects again – helping people. After four weeks the change was profound. He decided to come off the antidepressants (with his doctor's advice) and told me he was happier and more fulfilled than he had been for many years.

At this point it's important to state that I'm not a doctor and I would never dispense medical advice. Laughology is not a substitute for medically prescribed treatment and shouldn't be treated as such. What it does do, however, and what it did for Joe, is to offer a sustainable and achievable method to help individuals take control of certain aspects of their lives and develop resilience.

# MOOD HOOVERS

Not only is it important to know *what* makes you feel good but also *who* makes you feel good. Negative people not only have a deleterious effect on their own emotions and behaviour; they can also have a damaging influence on those around them. Individuals who take steps to surround themselves with positive people often find themselves adopting the attitudes of those around them. On the other hand, it can be very difficult to maintain a positive and happy outlook when you're surrounded by pessimists who look for the worst in any situation.

As well as your positive thinking triggers, it is important to take control of your life and recognise who makes you feel positive. We feed off the energies of others, so it's worth being aware of your own energy and the effect this has on other people. The way you feel is very important because it affects how you think, act and get along with others.

If you feel miserable and gloomy you tend to think of more sad things – you mope around, have no energy and don't feel like talking to others. This makes everyone around you feel fed up too. But when you feel happy you think about good things, smile a lot and feel lively and chatty. This makes everyone around you feel upbeat too.

Although this book is primarily about what makes us feel good, we also need to understand what has a negative effect on us. We can then learn to avoid those behaviours or, at the very least, understand how best to deal with them.

It may be that there are people in your life who drain your energy when you talk to them so you feel exhausted afterwards. I call these people *mood hoovers*. It can be difficult to deal with mood hoovers, especially if they are friends who have been in your life for a long time. You may feel you have a loyalty to listen to them, to be around them and to support them. However, while you are doing this you are not only having a negative impact on how you feel, but you are also sustaining their unconstructive behaviours. Of course it is important to be a good friend and listener – sometimes that is all we want. Nevertheless, if you see a pattern developing where someone only ever offloads negativity onto you or you avoid talking to certain people because of the impact they have on your mood, you have to ask yourself: do I want this person in my life? If the answer is yes, then ask yourself: why I am allowing them to do this to me and to themselves?

By always listening to this person you may think you are being a supportive friend. However, you are actually upholding their harmful behaviour by not challenging their negative thoughts, actions and patterns. You will be more of a friend if you challenge this aspect of their behaviour. Let them know what they are doing – perhaps they need help and support to break the damaging cycle/pattern. You don't have to be that support; in fact, in some cases it can be more productive to seek a well-structured approach from a professional.

Do help them with a positive action plan – such as contacting help groups or buying a book (I can highly recommend this one!) to help them change what is making them unhappy. But ultimately they have to do it themselves. If you find that after this they are still having a negative impact on your life, you need to really question how much time you spend with them if you want to continue the relationship and, if so, how it can be beneficial to you both. Perhaps you could agree that when you meet there has to be a certain amount of positive talk or maybe you could help them find their own laughter triggers.

 # INFECTIOUS EMOTIONS

Psychologists have found that if you put a pencil between your teeth while reading something you'll think the material funnier.[1] That's because your brain's interpretation is influenced by the smile on your face. If you sit up straight, instead of slouching, you'll feel happier too. The brain interprets things more positively when the mouth and spine are in positions that it recognises as positive behavioural responses.

In much the same way that we have behaviours, thoughts and people which help us laugh and feel positive, we have behaviours, thoughts and people which have the opposite effect. Just as laughter is contagious so too are moods, as Carl Jung observed in his studies on the

---

1    D. Eagleman, *Incognito: The Secret Lives of the Brain* (New York: Pantheon/Random House, 2011).

transference of emotions. In several studies moods have been shown to transmit from person to person, almost like a baton being passed from runner to runner in a relay race. Because of the way we communicate we pick up on facial expressions and slight changes in body language without even knowing it. And because we communicate how we feel, both consciously and subconsciously through verbal and non-verbal communication, we detect these changes and mimic them. This explains why, if you walk into a room after two people have had an argument, you may feel a bad atmosphere even if there is no evidence of that argument having occurred.

These messages have a powerful effect no matter how seemingly imperceptible they might be. In a study conducted by Dr Ellen Sullins, a psychologist at Northern Arizona University, two volunteers were asked to sit silently in a room waiting for the researcher to return.[2] The participants were chosen because of their opposing styles of expression: one was naturally animated and outgoing, the other was more subdued. When the researcher returned they were asked to fill out a questionnaire related to their mood. When their answers were analysed it transpired that the mood of the outgoing volunteer had transmitted to the introverted one. As they had not spoken, the assumption was that the good mood was communicated through body language.

## A PROBLEM SHARED IS A PROBLEM HALVED

We now know *what* your positive and laughter triggers are, but *who* are your positive trigger and laughter friends? Remember that you will have friends who are more than willing to help and support you, but sometimes we don't feel like bothering them or being a nuisance. Support networks are vital, so keeping a note of your feel-good friends will help when the time comes to call on someone.

---

2 E. S. Sullins, 'Emotional contagion revisited: effects of social comparison and expressive style on mood convergence', *Personality and Social Psychology Bulletin* 17 (1991), 166–174.

Write down all the people you can think of who make you feel good:

.............................................................

.............................................................

.............................................................

Now let's think about these people and what triggers they help to support.

Someone I can rely on in a crisis:

.............................................................

Someone who makes me feel good about myself:

.............................................................

Someone I can totally rely on:

.............................................................

Someone who will tell me how well or badly I am doing:

.............................................................

Someone I can talk to if I'm worried:

.............................................................

Someone who really makes me stop and think about what I am doing:

.............................................................

Someone who is lively:

.............................................................

Someone who makes me laugh hysterically:

.............................................................

Someone who finds me funny and I make them laugh:

.............................................................

Someone who introduces me to new ideas and concepts:

. . . . . . . . . . . . . . . . . . . . . . . . . . . . . . . . . . . . . . . . . . . . . . . . . . . . . . . . . . . . . .

When you think of your trigger friends consider their positive attributes. They should be people who are happy for you to be around them and who want to support you when you need a little extra help.

Our true friends are always prepared to help out and just talking to them can often make us feel better. Always remember that your attitude has an effect on others and how they respond to you. As well as individuals being positive laughter triggers for you, you can be a positive laughter trigger for them – it's a two-way street. Just as your friends are there for you to rely on, make sure they know you are there for them too. You don't have to be fun all the time; it is human nature to get down sometimes but good friends will support you when you're unhappy and help lift your mood. The important point to bear in mind is to know how to help yourself and to recognise when to stop talking about the problem and focus on the solution. Understand when to use your positive laughter triggers to enable you to help someone else and this will make you feel better too. We will cover this later in Chapter 6.

Over the next week try to smile more and laugh more. Notice how people around you smile back at you. If you feel good then you will spread happiness to others.

##  POINTS TO REMEMBER

- How you feel affects how others react to you.
- Mood is contagious – is yours worth catching?
- Be aware of the mood hoovers in your life.
- Don't get sucked into other people's negativity.

# CHAPTER 4

# THE POWER OF LAUGHTER

##  JUST WHAT THE DOCTOR ORDERED

I was working on a project with people who had long-term illness or had been diagnosed with a condition that would have a huge impact on their life. The idea was to look at how humour and laughter could be used to help cope with the everyday difficulties they faced dealing with their disease.

One man, who I'll call Jack, had testicular cancer and wanted to take part in the programme. When I spoke with him he was very keen to bring laughter and humour back into his life, not just for him but for his family too. He had two sons between the ages of 20 and 25 and talked about his relationship with them as being one of the most important and treasured parts of his life; it was one of the motivators that kept him strong. He divulged that his relationship with them had changed since his diagnosis. They had always shared a great sense of humour, often playing tricks and laughing together. He felt that because of his illness the humour within the family had taken a back seat and the boys weren't as forthcoming with jokes, possibly because they felt it would be inappropriate. But for Jack it was just what he needed.

Jack wanted to keep the humour going and for his sons to treat him exactly the same as before. I agreed to run some sessions with him and his family. It was not my job to tell them what to laugh at or to reveal that their father wanted to laugh with them more. Instead I explored humour and laughter with them in order to understand where it would come from naturally for them all. We had several sessions before Jack's operation and plenty of amusement was created. Jack reported that he felt closer to his sons again and the humour, some of it quite dark, was returning. After his operation I met with Jack. He told me that the night before his surgery he was feeling quite low and trying his hardest to stay positive. His sons had come to visit and make sure he was OK. They had brought a card with them and asked him to read it while they were there as they had chosen it carefully and felt the words were very special. When Jack opened the envelope the card read 'Sorry for the loss of your loved ones'! Jack loved the fact that his sons had brought in humour at that point, which for him showed that they still saw him as the same old dad – a man with a great sense of humour who was full of life – and that what was happening hadn't changed him at all. At that moment he said he felt OK and confident he could go forward and cope with his illness.

It is not for me to say whether this response was appropriate or inappropriate, but it was completely right for Jack and his sons at this time. It was unique to them and helped Jack feel better about the situation he was in. It may not be right for everyone (I certainly wouldn't have been so bold as to use this dark humour), but it clearly helped them all cope with the situation.

##  LAUGHTER – THE BEST MEDICINE

One of the most famous cases of laughter being used for medicinal purposes is that of journalist Norman Cousins. In the 1960s Cousins was diagnosed with ankylosing spondylitis, a life-threatening and painful condition that can cause the discs of the spine to fuse together. He was given six months to live but refused to give up hope. Due to his knowledge of psychology, from years of medical reporting, he believed in the power of the mind and positive thinking to improve his prognosis. He promptly discharged himself from hospital where he felt the environment and the attitude of some medical practitioners was not conducive to his overall well-being and treatment. Instead, Cousins checked himself into a hotel where he created a positive environment which he felt would help him get better.

Plenty of research has been written about negative emotions and their impact on well-being, but at the time there was no firm research into the beneficial effects of positive emotions on well-being and disease management. Cousins hypothesised that if negative emotions and stress could cause 'ill-being' then the opposite should be true. He set about prescribing for himself what at the time must have been one of the most unorthodox medical treatment programmes. It included Marx Brothers' movies, *Candid Camera* repeats and a strict rule that only positive, upbeat people could visit him. He wanted to encourage as much laughter and happiness around him as possible. He found that over time the more he laughed during the day the more pain-free sleep he had. In continuing to treat himself in this way he found the disease diminished and he was well enough to return to work. The self study became the basis for a best-selling book, *Anatomy of an Illness*.[1]

 # LAUGHTER'S IN THE BLOOD

Just in case you're not convinced, here's the science. Laughter and positive emotions help blood vessels function better, as shown by a study carried out at the University of Maryland School of Medicine in 2005.[2] Researchers looked at the effects of laughter on the endothelium, the inner lining of blood vessels, and found that it has a powerful effect on blood vessel tone. It also regulates blood flow and, in general, plays an important role in cardiovascular disease development. Lead researcher Dr Michael Miller said: 'it is conceivable that laughing may be important to maintain a healthy endothelium, and reduce the risk

---

1 N. Cousins, *Anatomy of an Illness as Perceived by the Patient: Reflections on Healing and Regeneration* (New York: Norton, 1979).
2 University of Maryland Medical Center, 'University of Maryland School of Medicine study shows laughter helps blood vessels function better' (7 March 2005). Press release available at http://www.umm.edu/news/releases/laughter2.htm (accessed 31 May 2012).

of cardiovascular disease'. In essence, the healthier the endothelium, the less chance there is of developing cardiac problems.

Researchers showed volunteers 15-minute segments of emotion-provoking films and afterwards ultrasound was used to measure what effect the film had on blood flow in the brachial artery (a major vessel in the arm used to measure blood pressure). They used clips from *Saving Private Ryan* (DreamWorks, 1998) to induce stress and *King Pin* (MGM, 1996) to provoke laughter. The study found that blood vessels dilated after funny films, increasing in diameter by 22%, therefore increasing blood flow. After watching clips from *Saving Private Ryan*, the same blood vessels decreased in diameter by 35%, thereby reducing blood flow. Which just goes to show, it's not always Oscar-winning films that are good for the heart!

Research has shown that the health benefits of laughter are far ranging. While more studies need to be done, investigations so far have shown that laughter can help to relieve pain, bring greater happiness and even increase immunity. A fairly new area of neuroscience called psycho-neuroimmunology (which combines psychology, neuroscience and immunology) studies the interactions between the brain and the immune system. Psychoneuroimmunological experiments are usually focused on stress and how this affects the nervous system and causes disease. In similar studies, laughter has been shown to cause changes in the autonomic nervous system, thereby reducing the level of stress hormones in the body, such as cortisol, epinephrine, adrenaline, dopamine and growth hormone. Too much stress and production of these hormones can cause a whole load of health issues including weight gain, heart strain and lack of sleep. However, endorphins – the hormones increased and released through laughter – help reduce stress hormones by acting as an antidote to them. Laughter also increases our neurotransmitter levels, which in turn give us improved sleeping patterns and feelings of happiness. Laughter can boost the number of antibody producing cells and enhances the effectiveness of T-cells which bolster our immune system. Put simply, studies suggest that laughter can help build a stronger immune system as well as lessening the physical effects of stress.

Laughter can also act as a physical release: it provides an emotional release, just as crying can. In some instances you may have cried and laughed hysterically, then felt better about a situation. This is your body's natural way of releasing tension. Laughter can act as a distraction from anger, stress and negative emotions and is a better and healthier diversion than drinking or smoking. A good belly laugh can also act as a workout for your tummy muscles, as a team at Stanford University found out. Professor William Fry, who led the study, found that laughter can provide a good cardiac workout and calls it 'internal jogging'. Fry, a professor of psychiatry who has devoted over 30 years of research to studying humour and laughter, explained; 'laughter improves circulation because it elevates the heart rate and blood pressure. A day's worth of hearty laughter, is about equal to ten minutes on the rowing machine.' [3]

Laughter exercises the diaphragm, contracts the abs and works out the shoulders, leaving muscles more relaxed afterwards. It even provides a good workout for the heart by working the cardiovascular muscles and pumping more blood and oxygen around the body.

There are social benefits to laughter too because it connects us with others. We all want to be around individuals who make us laugh and we love it when people laugh at our jokes or tales. It makes us feel accepted as part of the group. The more you let laughter into your life, the more likely it is that others around you will laugh too.

So let's sum up:

- Laughter provides enjoyable exercise, both toning and relaxing muscles.

- Laughter is a bit like an internal organ massage and leaves our insides feeling invigorated and alert.

- Laughter helps us stay healthy and even assists us in managing pain or illness.

- Laughter helps protect us from colds and viruses as it increases the levels of an antibody (Immunoglobulin A) in the nose and respiratory passages.

- Laughter increases levels of natural killer cells and antibodies to boost the immune system.

---

3   W. Fry, 'Mirth and the human cardiovascular system', in H. Mirdess and J. Turek (eds), *The Study of Humor* (Los Angeles, CA: Antioch University Press, 1979), pp. 56–61.

- Laughter stimulates the production of lymphocytes containing T-cells that fight cancer cells.
- Laughter reduces blood pressure and heart rate when practised regularly.
- Laughter engages every major system of the body.
- Laughter helps us feel good and look good (although not always at the same time!).
- Laughter oxygenates our blood.
- Laughter reduces the levels of the stress hormones epinephrine and cortisol.
- Laughter gives us perspective and encourages creative thinking.
- Laughter enhances problem-solving skills.
- Laughter brings us closer to other people.
- Laughter provides facial exercise and increases blood flow to the skin.
- Laughter activates our tear glands to brighten our eyes.

What more proof do you need that laughter and developing a sense of humour as a mood lifter is a great way of feeling better and living better? Remember, you can be in control of bringing on all these great physical effects from laughter.

 # FIND YOUR FUNNY BONE

Think about when you laugh and list below how it makes you feel. How does it make you feel about the people around you when you laugh with others? How does it make you feel after a bad day?

...........................................................................

...........................................................................

...........................................................................

Here is the outline of a person. Look at the shape of the body. Now, think of a physical effect of laughter and then draw a line to point out which part of the body it affects. Here are a few to start you off: smiling mouth, eyes scrunched up, belly wobbling … that's all I'm going to give you for now, so you get the idea!

Overleaf there is a longer list, but don't look at it yet – that's cheating! Think of as many physical effects of laughter as you can and the parts of the body they affect before you look.

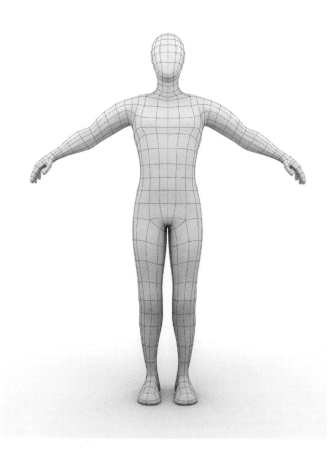

The physical effects of laughter might include:

- A change in brain chemistry – happy chemicals are released
- Scalp relaxes
- Head nods
- Eyebrows go up
- Eyes widen
- Eyes scrunch up
- Tears flow
- Nose crinkles
- Nose runs (snot – yuk!)
- Cheeks crease up
- Ears go back
- Face goes red
- Mouth opens
- Lips draw back into a smile
- Tongue sticks out
- Breath is expelled

- Coughing

- Spluttering

- Strange noises made (laughter!)

- Deep breaths drawn in

- Neck muscles relax

- Shoulders jump up and down

- Chest swells

- Lungs expand

- Oxygen intake increased

- Heart rate increases

- Heart muscles relax

- Blood vessels relax

- Belly wobbles

- Stomach muscles contract

- Farts (follow-through if you're really unlucky!)

- Hands grab stomach

- Bend at the waist

- A bit of wee pops out!

- Knees bend

- Toes curl

- The whole body rocks

Blimey! Bet you didn't realise how powerful laughter was! Now can you see how laughter exercises your whole body? It is just like going to the gym. So, the physical effects from laughter can create a positive response in the body as well as the mind.

Over the next week try this simple experiment with a group of friends. Say something funny or tell a joke. As they laugh, you start to laugh more. The more you laugh the more they'll laugh. Laughter is infectious! Over the next week deliberately seek out activities that make you laugh. Note how you feel after them, note how you sleep better and generally think better.

 # POINTS TO REMEMBER

■ Laughter has a great physiological impact on the body, helping you look healthier and happier on the outside and actually be healthier on the inside.

■ Laughter counteracts stress – if you are having a bad day look for something to laugh about.

■ Laughter is free and a more powerful medicine than any doctor can prescribe.

# CHAPTER 5

# WHAT IS HUMOUR?

 ## MUST HAVE GSOH

I tend to travel a lot delivering seminars and speaking at conferences. When I can I use the train as I find it less stressful than driving. I find trains relaxing and you can have a lot of fun watching other people. On this particular journey I was sitting opposite a man who can only be described as catalogue handsome. He was dressed to match and had style and charisma oozing out of him, not to mention cool. I caught his eye a couple of times and faintly smiled, while trying to act cool myself. Halfway through the journey I needed the toilet and as I walked past him I again shot him a smile.

There was a short queue and by the time I got in and waited for the automatic door to close slowly, I was so desperate I undid everything as fast as possible in order to relieve myself. In my hastiness I had forgotten to press the lock button on the door. Just as I had my pants round my ankles and was squatting over the toilet, the door started to open. I tried to reach over to press the close button again, but I was bound by my trousers and couldn't move fast enough. As the door slid back I could see it was the catalogue man. It was like being in a bad episode of *Blind Date*. I could tell by his face, as you so often could on *Blind Date*, that the reveal wasn't what he was looking for. In a desperate attempt to salvage some dignity, I thought I would test out my wit and said, 'Normally I get bought a drink first.' He had already pressed the close button and was repeatedly pressing it to try and cut short the scene. He muttered something about putting the lock on next time and walked off. He was not outside when I had finished, nor was he in the seat opposite me when I returned.

At the time, as you can imagine, it was highly embarrassing, but recounting the story to my friends, their laughter, or should I say hysteria, made me laugh too. I now feel very differently about what was a very awkward episode, but to this day it remains one of my laughter triggers. And I know now to always lock the door!

# HUMOUR PERSPECTIVE

Our sense of humour changes in different situations and no one can say that one person's humour is better than someone else's. It's about perspective, which changes all the time, and is dependent on what type of day we're having, our view of the situation and so on.

Austrian neurologist and psychiatrist Viktor Frankl was a Holocaust survivor who wrote about his experiences in a concentration camp and the relationships he formed with other prisoners in his book *Man's Search for Meaning*.[1] In this book Frankl draws on his professional expertise to analyse how he used humour during his experiences to make sense of the horrors going on around him.

One quote sums up the understanding of laughter and humour as a coping tool: 'Between stimulus and response there is a space. In that space is our power to choose our response. In our response lies our growth and our freedom.'

Humour as a way of dealing with terrible situations can be very personal and, at times, very dark (what is known as *gallows humour*). It offers us a way to process information that can help us move forward quickly. There is a lot of debate as to whether gallows humour in the medical and emergency services is acceptable, but who can judge on what is right or wrong for a particular individual? Most people would argue that the appropriateness of gallows humour depends entirely on the situation it is used in and the audience it is directed towards. There

---

1   V. Frankl, *Man's Search for Meaning* (Boston, MA: Beacon Press, 2006).

are many factors to consider: who is making the joke? What is their position in the situation? Are they the victim or perpetrator?

Coping with the traumatic incidents that medical staff and emergency workers see every day can be very difficult. There is always a danger that they get so caught up in the emotions of the situation that they are unable to remain professional and make objective decisions. Humour can be used as protective armour when performing their job; some people believe it helps them to make better and clearer decisions. There is relatively little academic research on gallows humour in medicine. From personal observations, and the little that has been written about it, it usually occurs amongst health care workers and seems to help them process serious, frightening or painful events in a light or satirical way.

A joke about a patient's condition told in front of the patient or their family would be improper and unethical because it has the potential to upset them; however, does a quip between doctors about a patient that the patient or family are not aware of actually harm anyone? Quite the opposite, it may assist doctors by helping them get through a terrible event and shift their state of mind quickly. In doing so it may enable them to give the next patient the best possible care.

In his 1927 essay 'Humour', Freud puts forth the following theory for the use of gallows humour: 'The ego refuses to be distressed by the provocations of reality, to let itself be compelled to suffer. It insists that it cannot be affected by the traumas of the external world; it shows, in fact, that such traumas are no more than occasions for it to gain pleasure.'[2] In short, we can use humour to help us control our emotions and move forward in difficult circumstances. Freud also observed that it is, very specifically, an act of defiance: 'By making our enemy small, inferior, despicable or comic, we achieve in a round-about way the enjoyment of overcoming him.'[3]

When using humour we should always be very aware of how we are using it and who we are with. Gallows humour is appropriate only at certain times, in certain places and with certain people. We must

---

2   S. Freud, 'Der Humor' (1927), *Almanach* (1928): 9–16.

3   S. Freud, *Jokes and Their Relation to the Unconscious* (1905), ed. and trans. J. Strachey. In *The Standard Edition of the Complete Psychological Works of Sigmund Freud*, vol. 8 (London: Hogarth Press/Institute of Psychoanalysis, 1960), pp. 8–236.

remember that humour is one of our most powerful tools and, as with any weapon, it can cause damage in the wrong hands. So, to address the delicate balance of offensive vs. funny in a way where we can enjoy the stress-relieving benefits of humour and laughter without the damaging effects of offensive jokes, we need a guide to help us think about appropriateness. It seems that it's not humour itself that is the problem, but the use of comedy to convey messages that are in themselves offensive. As such, I believe that some ground rules need to be established around humour. Here are my guidelines:

# HUMOUR RULES

- **Think of the message:** Ask yourself what the point is. Are you using humour to communicate something that you wouldn't say to someone without the joke attached? In which case don't say it. Humour should not be used as a get-out clause; it's all too easy to say 'I was only joking' when the message behind it was all too clear.

- **Know your audience:** If you're teasing someone are you sure you know them well enough to predict their reaction? Everyone's humour boundaries are different so bear this in mind before you speak out of turn.

- **Leave serious topics alone:** Don't joke about topics that might be controversial or painful to others, like death, physical disability, sexual harassment or racial inequality (or race in general).

- **Be careful of politics:** While a surprising number of comics make political jokes, it's very important to know your audience, so avoid making political jokes that might offend someone of a different ideology if they are part of the group.

- **If in doubt, leave it out:** If you're not sure how well a joke will be received, it's best not to tell it.

# THE HUMOUR PROCESS

We tend to think of humour as part of our genetic make-up, like blue eyes or big feet. But we're not born with our sense of humour – it is actually a learned thinking skill and behaviour that evolves and develops during childhood and is influenced by the people around us. Our behaviour and the things we say influence how others behave and respond to us. If we behave in a way others perceive as humorous, their response, which might be a smile or a laugh, will be understood as positive and it will reinforce the affirmative nature of that behaviour. This is how our sense of humour develops.

Humour can be the ability to recognise what makes something funny or a way of looking at a situation differently, as well as a state of mind that allows you to recognise that difference. Humour means you are able to alter your mood about situations – it is a form of emotional intelligence. Humour is not just about telling jokes and clowning around; it is also dependent on feelings. We may not see the humour in a situation as it happens because we are upset, stressed or anxious. Humour is about how we negotiate those feelings in relation to our interpretation of events and how we view them in relation to our world at that time.

If we want to be able to understand how to develop humour as a cognitive skill it is important to understand how humour works as a cognitive processing tool. Only then can we start to formulate a model for thinking and acting that will help us to consciously lift our mood, achieve good humour and enhance our sense of humour. As well as serving a social function, humour can be characterised as a cognitive process; for humour to occur, we need to interpret information in a creative way – often suspending logic – and thereby think differently about an event.

What causes us to perceive something as humorous has been a topic of much debate. Although humour takes many forms – including jokes, teasing, witty banter, slapstick and unintentional types of humour, such as slips of the tongue or someone slipping on a banana skin – it generally involves incongruity or the unexpected. Our understanding of the world creates a personal viewpoint and suddenly this is turned on its head in an absurd or strange way that causes the flexible thinking part of the brain – the prefrontal cortex – to manipulate ideas and activities so that they are perceived in opposite ways, such as real and unreal, important and trivial, threatening and safe. For example, why do we laugh when someone hides and jumps out at us? The act itself is usually startling and unexpected and when it happens we feel threatened because this is how the mind responds. However, almost immediately, when we realise there is no threat, we often laugh. This is because we have processed the information and realised that our perception of the threat is mistaken and therefore our reaction is incongruous.

Our perception of a threat can be different to a real threat. Finding perspective in these situations can help rationalise thinking and therefore prevent a reaction that could cause a negative outcome.

The prefrontal cortex is the most evolved part of the brain and helps to maximise our cognitive abilities. It is also the part of brain that is most sensitive to the effects of stress. Even mild stress can cause us to not think straight. Have you ever been in a stressful situation and forgotten the simplest information? This is a defence mechanism known as the fight-or-flight response. When our fight-or-flight response is activated, nerve cells fire and chemicals such as adrenaline, noradrenaline and cortisol are released into the bloodstream. All our energies and attention are focused on the perceived threat and we become prepared – physically and psychologically – to defend ourselves or run away. The brain's response is to react quickly so we can ignore everything else, including logic and reason, making it almost impossible to see past the threat. The danger is not always a physical one; in fact, in modern society this reaction is often prompted by stress caused through work or relationships.

By its very nature, the fight-or-flight system bypasses our rational mind, where our more well thought out beliefs, perspective and sense of humour reside. The threat of possible danger distorts our thinking and we narrow our focus to just those things that can harm us. The reason for pointing this out is that it is not just our thinking system that impacts on our humour but also our emotional system. If we are not in the right emotional place we cannot think rationally and open up to our flexible thinking; therefore to process information using the perspective of humour we have to be in the right emotional state too. Therefore using the techniques described earlier – in the first instance reaching a better emotional state by using your laughter triggers – you will then be able to develop your sense of humour to gain perspective and act and react better.

Humour and good mood often go hand in hand as humour can evoke a pleasant emotional response. Psychological studies have shown that exposure to humorous stimuli produces an increase in positivity and mood.[4] The emotional nature of humour is also clearly demonstrated by brain imaging research showing that exposure to humorous cartoons activates the well-known reward network in the limbic system of the brain.[5] The funnier a particular cartoon is rated by a participant, the more strongly these parts of the brain are activated. From other research we know that these same brain circuits underlie pleasurable emotional states associated with a variety of enjoyable activities

4   A. Szabo, 'The acute effects of humor and exercise on mood and anxiety', *Journal of Leisure Research* 35 (2003), 152–162.
5   D. Mobbs, M. D. Greicius, E. Abdel-Azim, V. Menon and A. L. Reiss, 'Humor modulates the mesolimbic reward centers', *Neuron* 40 (2003), 1041–1048.

including eating, listening to music, sexual activity and mood-altering drugs.

This explains why humour is so pleasing and why people go to such lengths to experience it as often as they can; whenever we laugh at something funny, we are experiencing an emotional high that is rooted in the biochemistry of our brains. It can therefore be argued that humour is essentially an emotion that is elicited by particular cognitive processes. So humour and mood are linked, which means we can use one to affect the other and by learning a 'humour process' we can alter mood and, to a degree, channel our thoughts into focusing on a more constructive outcome and behaviour.

Understanding the humour process helps us build a cognitive and behavioural model that enables perspective and proactive thinking. Some studies suggest that, on a simple level, the complex process involves three main brain components: a cognitive thinking part which helps you get the joke; a second part which governs movement and stimulates the muscles of the face to smile and laugh; and a third emotional part which helps produce the happy feelings that accompany a mirthful experience.

 # SEEING THE FUNNY SIDE

There are times in everyone's life when, if you look back afterwards, you find it funny but at the time it was not. This is because your perspective changes over time. Write down any examples of situations that have made you laugh, but only after the event happened.

......................................................................

......................................................................

......................................................................

For example, my partner and I decided to take up salsa dancing lessons. While I had some dancing experience my partner had none and the situation was totally alien to him. During the lesson he became increasingly frustrated and his flight-or-fight mechanism kicked in, which made it even more difficult for him to concentrate and he nearly left the lesson. After the session (some time afterwards) we chatted about what had happened and his response to it. With the benefit of perspective, and with his prefrontal cortex now fully engaged, he could see the absurdity of his reaction and we fell about laughing. He is now a champion salsa dancer. (OK, so that bit is exaggerated but only for comic effect!)

Recognising events like these as funny can help you deal with similar experiences in the future. We will go into this theory and practice more, in Chapter 8. For now just think of as many situations as possible.

Now think about other times where your fight-or-flight mechanism has been activated – where you didn't see the funny side. Write them down below. Is there a way you can view them differently? Of course, there will be some situations where you are not able take a different viewpoint and it is perfectly natural to have sad and negative emotions as well. But when you can find a different perspective, working to enhance this can be helpful.

........................................................................................

........................................................................................

........................................................................................

 # POINTS TO REMEMBER

- You can train yourself to have a sense of humour.

- If something seems bad at the time you can imagine yourself laughing about it later.

- Humour is a coping mechanism as well as a social tool.

- Perspective is subjective; in certain situations it may be best not to laugh out loud.

# CHAPTER 6

# THE MECHANICS
# OF HUMOUR

 ## FUNNY OR FAUX PAS?

Comedians often have trouble switching off their internal censor. If there's a possible laugh to be had, no matter how inappropriate, a stand-up will feel the urge to blurt it out. It's like hurdling a social barrier – you are never too sure what is on the other side or whether your outburst will be met with laughter or revulsion. Knowing whether a seemingly inappropriate joke will work or not is an art that comedians learn through trial and error. It becomes instinctive. A good stand-up will be able to read a room and gauge what level of humour will appeal to a specific audience.

Several years ago I was asked to compère a comedy night for a small cancer charity in the north-west of England. A friend of a friend had overcome cancer and had organised the event to raise money for the charity which had helped her. It was attended by a mixed group who all had some link to the charity. Many of the people in the audience were cancer sufferers and survivors.

I was on stage, running through my routine and introducing the comics who would be appearing through the evening. Part of my job was also to encourage people to buy tickets for the raffle.

'Throughout the night we'll also be holding a raffle for cancer …'

That's when the joke popped into my head. Normally it would have seemed in bad taste but instinctively I knew that many people in the audience would see the funny side.

'… crap prize, I know, but there will be better prizes later.'

Momentarily the room went quiet while the audience worked out if they were allowed to laugh. I imagine people were trying to establish whether the joke was making fun of cancer, which it wasn't; it was about the simultaneous juxtaposition of cancer and comedy. The joke was well received, especially by those who had been affected by cancer. This isn't surprising as many people who suffer from life-threatening illnesses find relief in humour.

In 1995, breast cancer survivor Christine Clifford set up the Cancer Club which offers support and relief to cancer patients and their families through the use of humour and shared experience. In her book *Not Now … I'm Having a No Hair Day* she often emphasises the benefits of humour for individuals suffering with chronic illness, making the point that it's not people with long-term diseases such as cancer, that lose their sense of humour, but avoidance of the subject by others, for fear of saying the wrong thing.[1] This only proves to make the person feel more isolated and uncomfortable with their prognosis. Use of humour can normalise a situation and put everyone involved at ease, as described in the story in Chapter 4 of my own experience of working with a gentleman with testicular cancer. It was a relief to him when his nearest and dearest were able to find and share humour with him, which made him feel normal and normalised the difficult situation he was going though.

---

1   C. Clifford, 'As simple as A, B, C' (February 2002). Available at http://www.thebreast-caresite.com/tbcs/CommunitySupport/FunnyYouMentionItPage/AsSimpleAsABC.htm (accessed 31 May 2012).

#  HUMOUR – NOT JUST FOR LAUGHS

How you choose to respond to something – your behaviour – can be the difference between creating a positive or negative outcome. Our response is often so quick we don't even think about it, we just react. Humour helps us to detach emotionally and find perspective. When we do this we can be proactive rather than reactive. Being in good humour is a state of mind, and that state of mind has a huge impact on how we feel, how we interpret events and how we behave and respond.

Taking the time to view a situation positively creates an optimistic mood and allows us to become 'good humoured'. This isn't always easy to do, however, as our feelings can often override our logical thought processes. For example, if you feel angry with someone, at the height of that anger it is a real skill to be able to take a step back and find a different perspective to change your emotional state, using humour or even employing your laughter triggers. Sometimes walking away and giving yourself time to cool down is the best course of action.

It is important to remember that humour isn't always an appropriate response. When we use humour as an internal coping mechanism to affect a shift in our personal state, we must also recognise that its context in the external world is just as important. When you are in the heat of an argument, using humour internally to diffuse your own negative feelings can be an effective method to change your perspective and take control of the situation. However, it's not always advisable to laugh out loud or make a humorous remark that could be construed as sarcastic.

As we have seen, the way we feel affects our sense of humour and humour affects the way we feel; the two are intrinsically linked and work together. Consider a situation where everyone is joking around and having a laugh. If you're in a good mood, in 'good humour', you join in and laugh with them because you're in the right state of mind. At other times you're not in the right state of mind, for whatever reason – you've had a hard day at work, you've had a trying morning with your family or you've had some bad news. You're not in the right condition to want to join in with the fun.

What we traditionally view as humour – comedy, jokes, entertainment – can occur when the unexpected happens to challenge our perception of the world. In addition, humour can be a learnt skill in order to gain a different perspective at those times when we need to question the way we think about a situation in order to find a way forward. Most people think of humour as something that exists just for the sake of entertainment or for adding spice to social occasions. In fact, it is a fundamental aspect of the human mind and, as such, is part of a system for information processing which we can influence to our advantage. The Association for Applied and Therapeutic Humor call this 'therapeutic humour'. In this sense humour can help us to:

- See things from many perspectives other than the most obvious.

- Be spontaneous.

- Create positive mood and outlook.

- Grasp unconventional ideas or ways of thinking.

- See beyond the surface of things.

- Enjoy and participate in the playful aspects of life.

- Not take ourselves too seriously.

Having a good sense of humour is considered one of the most important characteristics of happy and successful people. It helps you to solve problems, improve relationships and develop a positive outlook on virtually every aspect of your life. People often talk about having a good sense of humour but rarely have they considered what this really means.

So far we have defined humour as having a different perspective on things and described how it can be used to help in certain situations. However, it also has the potential to have a deeper and even more powerful impact. Where appropriate you can use humour to help change your perspective on past events. This can mean going back through your life and looking at your belief systems – how they developed, what elements went into making them and what behaviours continue to support them. It's not a simple process but Laughology aims to simplify it and help you develop a 'humour toolkit' that will enable you to understand where your perspectives and reactions are having an adverse effect.

Laughology is not about going through life and laughing things off or never taking a moment to cry or reflect on how something makes you feel. Nor am I suggesting that you ignore a problem and don't take it seriously. It is about being able to move forward from a predicament by enabling more positive thinking, thereby improving problem-solving and producing a more positive state of mind, which then leads to a more constructive outcome.

The idea behind the toolkit is that humour offers a sense of perspective and allows you to remove yourself emotionally from a troubling thought or position. Most of us have the tendency to believe that any problem we are confronting at a particular moment is the most important thing that is going on in the world. It can take over our mind and thoughts and become all encompassing, not allowing for any positive emotion or solution-focused thinking.

Looking at a problem in this way can make you feel as if it is everywhere and it becomes the focus of your whole being. A developed sense of humour is important in allowing you to think outside of the problem and to step aside from it, which in turn gives you a new perspective.

A cancer patient described the role of humour in his life in this way:

The other reactions; anger, depression, suppression, denial, took a little piece of me with them. Each made me feel just a little less human. Yet laughter made me more open to ideas, more inviting to others, and even a little stronger inside. It proved to me that, even as my body was devastated and my spirit challenged, I was still a vital human.[2]

An important part of a developed sense of humour is the capacity to take *yourself* lightly, not just the situation you are in. Even though you may take your work or your problem very seriously, humour can be

---

2   S. Burton, 'Why not laugh?' Available at http://www.sburton.com/whynotlaugh.htm (accessed 31 May 2012).

used to help you become resilient, to change your emotional state and feel better.

# HUMOUR AND THE BRAIN

| Humour and laughter break negative thought patterns... | ...when we think about a situation in a positive light... | ...we make better decisions which impact on behaviour |

The term *humour* derives from the medicine of the ancient Greeks, who believed that a mix of fluids in the body, known as 'the four humours', created balance for health and well-being. An imbalance would have a harmful effect on health and cause disease. Although medicine has moved on from this understanding we still consider health and emotion to be linked.

A variety of theories have been put forward through the ages to explain why we use humour. Freud described humour as our strongest defence mechanism which allows us to face problems and avoid negative emotions. Defence mechanisms are automatic and often sub-conscious psychological processes that protect us against anxiety. If we are in a situation that threatens to overwhelm us emotionally and we don't know how to respond, humour can step in as a safety mechanism, almost like a default setting. On a more conscious level we use humour to deflect stressful situations. Children and young people are very good at doing this; for example, clowning around when they find school lessons too difficult.

Humour can also be used to gain a sense of superiority – we exploit it to judge a person or situation as inferior in order to make ourselves feel better. Taken to its extreme this use of humour can be destructive; however, it also explains more innocent amusement, such as why we laugh at people falling over or programmes of mishaps and blunders, such as *You've Been Framed!* As human beings we naturally like to position ourselves in society and our survival instincts tell us that it is best to be superior. Therefore if you see someone doing something that makes you feel better about your life and your interpretation of the world, or at the very least normalises it, this feeds into your understanding of where you fit in the world and makes you feel good about yourself and your situation.

More often than not we are expected to confirm to certain conventional behaviours. The relief theory of humour suggests that comedy focused on inappropriate and socially unacceptable behaviours is perceived as funny because it affords us relief from those constraints. This is why some near-the-knuckle comedians, such as Frankie Boyle, are so popular and why after many tragic news events bad-taste jokes begin to circulate. This theory also explains why humour can occur in stressful or sad situations such as funerals; it can offer relief during difficult times.

According to Freud, we all have an internal 'censor' which prevents us from projecting our natural impulses and this helps us to become civilised and socially aware. When we disarm this censor using humour it allows us to indulge in forbidden thoughts. The relief comes from breaking down this internal conflict and, in the case of comedy clubs, normalising your illicit thoughts.

Another theory, the incongruity theory, proposes that we find humour in unexpected things or events. We have a set of beliefs about how the world works and how things behave in it. If this is challenged or the unexpected happens, we are shocked and don't process the information as normal. This shock response can often be externalised as laughter because the brain does not compute the event and therefore does not know how to respond.

# IT'S NOT AS BAD AS IT SEEMS

Let's put this to the test. Much like we did earlier, can you think of a situation that you didn't find funny at the time, but that you were able to see the amusing side of when recalling it a few days, weeks, months or years later (depending on how bad it was!)?

Write down below what this was. If you can't recollect one of your own, think of an example that a friend or family member has shared with you. The important part of this exercise is to find a story that in hindsight became funny when re-told. You can even speak to someone about an experience and use it here. Listen to how they talk about it and ask why it appears funny now, but not at the time.

.................................................................

.................................................................

.................................................................

To gain the ability to use our humour perspective in a proactive way, we need to analyse how the process works. When the story is recalled, what made it funny? Was it shocking or unexpected? What elements of the situation were comic? Were they exaggerated?

Go through the story again and highlight points that were amusing. Understanding and learning from experiences like this will help you to find perspective in future situations. Remember the theories discussed earlier and, in situations where it is appropriate, relate these to the story you have written down above. Awareness of this in day-to-day life can help you regain logic and control in situations where you begin to feel overwhelmed. This exercise encourages you to think about how you want to act rather than simply reacting emotionally, thereby allowing for a more positive state of mind when faced with life's challenges.

# PAYING INTO THE HUMOUR BANK

One way to gather more humour is to have what I call a 'bank of good humour' and pay into it. Think of it like a bank in your brain where, instead of keeping money, you store your humour. Like any bank, if you haven't got anything in your account you can't make any withdrawals. The same applies to humour. If you don't make regular 'humour payments' you won't have enough to keep your account in credit.

So how do you keep your balance healthy? Making deposits into your humour bank is about accumulating positivity – looking for things you find funny, laughing, being happy and being grateful. Paying in regularly will have the effect of helping you see life in a more glass half-full way. It's not just about telling jokes all the time, making light of things or going out and having a laugh, although this is also important; it's about looking much deeper. For example, think about the place where you work. Is there a colleague there who is full of negativity and who tries to inflict those destructive attitudes on everyone else? How do you react to and interact with that person? If you go along with their negativity you will feel pessimistic as well. If you choose to counteract that negativity with positivity, and not be drawn into their pessimism but instead offer a more constructive way to look at the situation, with a smile, you have paid into your humour bank.

Other simple ways to 'bank' humour include remembering your own funny stories, watching comedy films and collecting humorous pictures, cartoons and sayings. Another way is to keep a humour diary. At the end of each day list the things that made you laugh, smile and feel good. The very act of writing them down and recalling amusing observations of the day will reinforce them in your mind and help you enhance your humour perspective. Periodically read back through your diary, just so you remember how much pleasure there is in life. You may feel this is impractical, that you have nothing to be happy about or that you don't have the time to devote to a diary. In the case of the former, everyone can find joy in something – a sunset, a warm day, the sound of children laughing. If you actively look for things that make you laugh and feel happy, the chances are you will find them. If you feel you are too busy to write down your thoughts, perhaps start each day with a few brief moments of reflection where you are thankful for the things you have. Identify one or two things you are grateful for, such as your health or your family. You'll be amazed how much of a shift you will find in your attitude and how positive you will feel just by doing this.

Take responsibility for your happiness, recognise what makes you laugh and go out and find the things that do. What you put into your mind you get out, and therefore if you pay in fun, laughter and positivity, then that's what you'll get out.

Now let's do a quick humour bank audit:

1    On a scale of 1 to 10 how often do you take time to pay into your humour bank?

2    How can you improve this by just 2 points?

3    What simple things could you do that you can start doing today?

You can use this audit at the end of each day: think about how your day went on a scale of 1 to 10 (with 10 being great). If it was a 4 or 5, how could you have done things differently using Laughology techniques that would help you feel better should this happen again? You don't even need to write this down; just think it through before you go to sleep to help you become a more solution-focused and happy thinker.

 # POINTS TO REMEMBER

■ Humour gives you perspective.

■ If your personal coping mechanism is humour, it's OK to laugh about difficult situations.

■ Humour can be found in the most unexpected places.

■ You can't always control what you find funny.

```
Humour is the healthy way of feeling a
'distance' between one's self and the problem,
a way of standing off and looking at one's
problem with perspective.
```
                                                    Rollo May

# CHAPTER 7

# YOUNG AT HEART

Humor is one of the most serious tools we have
for dealing with impossible situations.

Erica Jong

##  FINDING GABBY'S GIGGLE

The first time I met Gabby I was in a library in the north of England – she was attending a workshop I was running about Laughology. Gabby was with her mum, Julie, and they had come to find out more about how Laughology could potentially help with Gabby's situation. She had been diagnosed with schizophrenia and was having treatment to help her cope with the challenges she was facing.

The first thing that struck me about Gabby was that she was withdrawn and lacked confidence. She even found it hard to maintain eye contact when talking to me. Julie described their situation and we stayed in the library after the session chatting about what Gabby wanted. Gabby explained how she felt and what the condition had done to her confidence and self-esteem and how it had taken away her independence. She was only 19 and felt that for the past two years of her illness she hadn't had anything to be happy about and hadn't laughed. Julie said that before the illness Gabby had a great sense of humour and was fun to be around, adding that one of the main things she missed hearing from Gabby was her giggle.

I agreed to think about everything Julie and Gabby had told me and said I would be in touch about possibilities the following week. I put a lot of thought into what to do next as I really wanted to help Gabby and needed to be clear about the best way to do this. From speaking to her it was clear that one of the most important things she wanted was to be able to laugh again – she hadn't felt this carefree feeling for a long time. So I decided this would be my focus and I put together a pro-gramme which would be specific to her and her needs. I called it 'Finding Gabby's Giggle'.

I met with Gabby once a week over the next two months. We worked on various exercises, similar to the ones you will find in this book, and I used lots of visual stimuli too. By the third week Gabby was making more eye contact with me and was confident enough to attend ses-sions without her mum. On the fourth week I brought in some silly pictures I had taken from the internet and when Julie joined us the pair had great fun coming up with captions for them – these could be ridiculous, true or funny as long as they went with the photo. The penultimate picture was one of the Queen with her finger up her nose. Without pausing, Gabby shouted out 'Snotty Royals'. It was the best caption I had ever heard for that picture!

At that point Gabby fell about laughing and didn't stop, which caused Julie and me to start. Gabby had found her giggle again! We continued the sessions after this, working on confidence and self-esteem. Gabby reflected on the session at the end of the programme and said that the laughter made her feel 'normal' again. She felt better – good about herself. When she felt happy and good she also felt more confident and recognised herself again. Gabby continued to make progress and, with the help of her mum and other support, started living by herself again. She said this was due to her finding her giggle. Using Laughology allowed Gabby to step away from the seriousness of her situation and adopt a carefree attitude and outlook. This almost child-like state gave her freedom from the constraints of her illness.

Using these techniques in everyday situations helps us to think more freely about the world and any problems that arise in it, rather than dwelling on some of the more negative strategies we have learnt as adults.

# DISCOVERING YOUR INNER CHILD

Did you know that babies and toddlers laugh up to 300 times a day, while adults, on average, laugh only 17 times a day? What went wrong? How did we misplace our gift for humour?

We seem to lose our ability to laugh as the years advance. Do you remember laughing and playing as a kid – not having to worry about bills, the mortgage, the future? Do you recollect using your imagination to create anything you wanted – making up fun plays, skipping in the street and not caring what others thought about you? Maybe that's where the problem lies as we grow older – we start to care about other people's opinions too much. This can hold us back from doing things because we want to fit in and because society says that as adults we should work rather than play. As George Bernard Shaw said: 'We don't stop playing because we grow old; we grow old because we stop playing.'

As we grow older we get taught that work and play are two separate things, and that play can't occur until the work is done. As a result of this conditioning we learn to compartmentalise the concepts of work and play into separate categories. I am a firm believer in rules and boundaries with children, but why can't eating, chores and homework be fun too? If they were presented in this way I imagine you would get a lot more done and your children would be more engaged in the task.

If you spend any time watching a child you soon notice that work and play are inseparable. There is no distinction between them in the child's mind – it's how they learn, explore and cope with challenges. As children play, they learn to solve problems, get along with others and develop the motor skills needed to grow and develop.

Play is as important to our physical and mental health as getting enough sleep, eating well and exercising. Play teaches us how to manage and transform our 'negative' emotions and experiences. It supercharges learning, helps to relieve stress and connects us to others and the world around us. Play can also make work more productive and pleasurable.

Our brains are hard-wired for play and imagination. We need play as babies, as children and as adults. Given the opportunity, adults take up sports, musical instruments and play games. Despite the power of play, somewhere between childhood and adulthood, many of us stop playing. We exchange play for work and responsibilities. When we do have some leisure time, we're more likely to zone out in front of the TV or computer rather than engage in creative and brain-stimulating play. By giving ourselves permission to play with the joyful abandon of childhood, we can continue to reap its benefits throughout life.

Play is a catalyst: it helps to transform ideas and develop practice. Nature has selected play as a trait for competitive advantage. If we can re-establish this practice in adulthood, we can rediscover that sense of wonderment and possibility that we had as children, which can lead to hope and positivity.

# CHILD'S PLAY

As we have seen, as we get older we tend to forget how vital play is as a tool, both physical and cognitive. Cognitive play – using our imagination – is intricately connected with how humour is formed. As we grow we use our imagination to explore solutions to problems and make sense of the world. This develops our sense of humour and helps us to cope with difficult situations. So why do we grow out of this positive habit?

There is a branch of science that may be able to answer these questions. The study of juvenile traits, both physical and mental, is called neoteny. The area we are concerned with here is *psychological neoteny*, a phrase coined by Bruce Charlton, Professor of Theoretical Medicine at the University of Buckingham. He explains how people displaying childlike or neotenous aspects of their personalities can have advantages in modern life, like being able to adapt quickly, make friends, think outside the box and come up with new and exciting concepts. These thinking traits and behaviours related to child-like attitudes happen because in a neoteny state, as outlined above, social boundaries and rules don't apply as much. With children, anything is possible because they have not learnt or been influenced by pessimistic and, let's face it at times, realistic constraints. If you take a cardboard box into a room full of children, that cardboard box can be a train, a car or a door to another world. They see it, they believe it; they use their imagination. Imagination is the key to thinking differently. Without it the world would not move on. We need to hone this skill as it's a vital ingredient to humour.

Unfortunately, as we become adults, social pressures and constraints – the idea of needing to be serious to get on – lead us to suppress these neotenous attributes. How many times have you heard a youngster told, 'Oh, stop being a big baby – just grow up!' However, taking on the mantle of adult responsibility shouldn't have to mean rejecting the child in us. Childlike qualities such as playfulness and creativity are positive attributes for adults too, helping us to problem-solve and cope with difficulties with greater perspective. Developing your playful side can enhance your ability to think in more positive ways.

Many scientists who have contributed great things to the world are said to have had neotenous traits, including Alexander Fleming and Albert Einstein. As Thomas Armstrong explains in his book *Awakening Genius in the Classroom,* 'Einstein brought a childlike disposition to looking at space and time into his powerful adult mind (a wonderful example of neoteny), and our view of the universe was never the same again.'[1]

Einstein was known for his playful attitude and child-like behaviours, often pulling funny faces when expected to be serious.

---

1  T. Armstrong, *Awakening Genius in the Classroom* (London: Atlantic Books, 1998).

Being able to switch on your neotenous traits means freeing up your mental agility and flexibility. As children we have yet to build up the beliefs that form our fears, stressors and anxieties; we approach the world with a sense of excitement and use our imagination to learn, laugh and play. Humour suspends reality and allows for imagination, perspective, fun, playfulness, mental agility, creativity, emotional intelligence, resilience and much more. These are the same qualities we find in neoteny – qualities that allow us to function more effectively in work, life and relationships.

As comic and humorist Steve Allen said: 'I've always been aware of the child in me. Humour, especially the best of it, is very childish. It can be wise, philosophically valuable, or helpful to the world. But childishness is one of the marvellous things about being human.'[2]

According to the science of neoteny, our brains have evolved to continue playing; the retention of youthful attitudes and behaviours into later adulthood is actually a valuable developmental characteristic. And there is a correlation between intelligence and play. Play has huge intellectual benefits: it has been shown to stimulate the amygdala, an area in the brain related to emotions and memory, thereby increasing positive emotional responses. It also promotes prefrontal cortex development, which is where cognition happens, so it can help to develop emotional maturity and improve decision-making and problem-solving.

 ## REDISCOVERING PLAY

List here all the things you loved doing when you were younger (games like hide-and-seek, building dens, etc.):

.........................................................................

.........................................................................

.........................................................................

---

2   Quoted in A. Snowden Crosman, *Young at Heart: 61 Extraordinary Americans Tell How to Defy Age with Zest, Work and Healthy Lifestyles*, rev. edn (Bothell, WA: Book Publishers Network, 2005).

How often do you get to do these activities now or what do you do in your life instead that has the same amount of enjoyment? List these here:

.................................................................................

.................................................................................

.................................................................................

If you feel you don't do many such activities, what would you like to do? Write a list below and use your imagination – don't let reality get in the way for now.

.................................................................................

.................................................................................

.................................................................................

Out of all these things, pick your top three that you would really like to pursue:

1 ..............................................................................

2 ..............................................................................

3 ..............................................................................

Now write down what you can do to make this happen as if there were no boundaries. What would be the very first step? A phone call? Stepping outside the door? Going on the internet to find out more information? Contacting a friend?

.................................................................................

.................................................................................

.................................................................................

This is how children think naturally. Allowing ourselves to reflect in this way helps us to find solutions. It helps your brain move forward without the edits we have learnt to add as we get older. Successful people often have these traits and use this quality in vision-building exercises. Once you have made a pathway in your imagination it helps you find that pathway in reality. The important thing is to keep taking the steps to get there. You can use this technique of childlike thinking to move forward in lots of different situations.

It is really important to make time for you and to do the things that you enjoy. These can be activities that are just for you or that you do with someone else, but knowing what these are and making time for them is essential to feeling better and happier.

# POINTS TO REMEMBER

- Don't underestimate the power of play.

- Make time for the things you enjoy doing – you're never too old to try playing.

- Is your work balanced with enough play and imagination time? Do you need to make time at work for fun and imaginative play?

- When life gets too serious take some time out to do something fun – you'll feel better and find solutions.

- Childlike thinking is good thinking. Do act your shoe size, not your age – sometimes it's the way forward.

# CHAPTER 8

# IMPROVE YOUR LIFE WITH LAUGHOLOGY

 ## SMILING INSIDE

When I first met Cathy she was withdrawn, isolated and a sectioned patient in a secure mental health unit. She had been in and out of secure units for much of her life. She was medicated and had been placed on a psychiatric rehabilitation programme. As part of this programme I was engaged to run a pilot module using Laughology to try and help a selected group of patients. Cathy had previously undergone a variety of therapies including empathy therapy, anger management and cognitive-behavioural therapy. She told me that none of them had worked for her. From what she said, I concluded that she had given up all faith in the treatments she had been prescribed.

In the first group session Cathy approached me and explained that she had come along only as a spectator; she had no intention of joining in and was attending 'to get off the wing for a bit'. When I began the sessions I insisted that staff as well as patients participated to improve relationships between the two groups. The long-term goal was to create a more positive environment and to indentify and train a select number of staff and patients within the facility who would become Laughology facilitators. They would continue promoting Laughology techniques after the pilot had finished.

Despite Cathy's reticence, in the first session I noticed that there were a few activities which seemed to spark her interest; in particular, the exercises in which I encouraged the group to think about positive laughter triggers. I realised Cathy had a keen sense of humour as well as a desire to be happy. As the sessions went on, I asked her to contribute and most times she would refuse initially. However, there always came a point where suddenly she would interject with a positive and valuable comment. It was almost as if, despite convincing herself that nothing would work for her, she couldn't help enjoying the sessions.

In the third session I had a 'eureka' moment. We were doing a practical, fun exercise in pairs which was designed to encourage laughter. I looked over at Cathy who had needed a lot of encouragement just to take part and I saw her break into a fit of giggles. Until that moment she had been emotionally detached, almost as if part of her personality was absent. But there, in that room, she came alive and a sparkle lit up her eyes. Cathy was actually enjoying herself – something that hadn't happened for a long time.

Following this breakthrough, the change was monumental. In each subsequent session Cathy came in with a joke or a funny anecdote about her week. She even arrived with an enthusiastic smile. Staff noticed the difference in her too and commented to me on how much she had changed.

Throughout the pilot participants were encouraged to evaluate their progress. Cathy said that although she'd undergone a lot of therapy in her life, it had always been done 'to her' and Laughology was the only one which she had chosen to do herself. 'If I had to choose again, I know which one I would go for first,' she said. 'This is the only thing which has actually made me feel better.'

Different therapies work for different people and I'm not saying Laughology is the only answer. But what it did for Cathy, and for many other people in various walks of life, is to allow them to realise that they can feel good. Once this realisation is made, they can focus on the behaviours that will help them to continue to feel good.

# A FRAMEWORK FOR LAUGHOLOGY

So far we've looked at what makes us laugh and how our sense of humour develops. This is the science that underpins the Laughology model. Understanding how we process information and react to situations, which in turn affect our mood, can help us to put in place new cognitive tools for feeling better during challenging times. The basis for this way of changing behaviours is grounded in the discipline of cognitive-behavioural therapy (CBT).

CBT helps people to achieve changes in the way that they think, feel and behave. It is based on the idea that some ways of thinking and behaving can trigger or fuel certain mental states, such as depression. A CBT therapist can help you to understand your thought patterns and behaviours and to identify any harmful, unhelpful or false ideas/ thoughts that could lead to such states of mind. The aim is then to shift your behaviour and thinking to avoid those ideas and also to enable your thought patterns to become more realistic and helpful.

As we've seen in previous chapters, behaviours have an impact on mood. If we laugh, smile or draw on laughter triggers we feel better about things – we feel happier. This works because our brain analyses events and behaviours and assigns to them certain moods, thoughts and feelings based on how we have reacted to similar events in the past. It links behaviours to moods. The part of the brain that links cognition to action is called the supplementary motor. In recent years it has come under increasing scrutiny from cognitive neuroscientists, motor physiologists and clinicians.

This process also explains the psychological mechanics of phobias. Take arachnophobia for example. If you believe spiders are scary (as I do) your behaviour when you see a spider reinforces this. Your body goes into fight-or-flight mode, your pulse races, your palms sweat and you get short of breath. This reaction reinforces the belief that Incy Wincy is terrifying. Your reaction is to leave the room where the spider is. When you do your pulse rate settles, the fear subsides and you calm down. Your behaviour has reaffirmed that running away from spiders is positive and, because you feel better about being away from the spider, it also reinforces the belief that they are scary. To break this loop therapists often use what is known as exposure therapy: the patient is encouraged to face their fear, thereby changing their behaviour both physically and psychologically.

For the purposes of Laughology, it helps to understand a little about the mechanics of CBT and how behaviours and feelings interact with one another because this will help you start to identify and challenge behaviours and thoughts that impact on your moods. You will then be able to recognise the things you are doing that perpetuate negativity and begin to counteract these or change them using the power of laughter and a humour perspective, which we know has huge positive effects. You can also alter your mood by developing different ways of thinking and acting in various situations. This is what is known in Laughology as the 'good humour toolkit'; it is a way for you improve your mood and feel better. As discussed earlier, laughter taps into our behaviour both physically and psychologically, instantly changing the way we feel. As a cognitive process, humour can also help to alter and enhance mood. By developing these two as a toolkit we can learn to use laughter and humour as a life skill.

 ## WHY LAUGHOLOGY WORKS

CBT is where psychology and the biological functioning of the brain meet. By consciously employing techniques, such as CBT, and other psychotherapeutic approaches, we can alter the instinctive, learnt and subconscious workings of our brain – it's almost like having an over-ride switch. Once we understand how to do this, it's a pretty cool thing to do. There is still a great deal we don't understand about how the brain works, but we're gradually finding out how we can affect it with our own thinking and behaviours.

In tests, the brain scans of individuals suffering from depression show an abnormally low level of activity in a part of the brain called the prefrontal cortex (the cognitive part of the brain). The more depressed the subject, the less active this part of the brain was. The prefrontal cortex is where humour processing predominantly occurs; therefore developing your humour skills will increase activity here and potentially aid the production of chemicals for happiness.

The prefrontal cortex is known to have numerous connections with other parts of the brain that are responsible for controlling three neurotransmitters that are important in mood regulation: dopamine, epinephrine and serotonin. Dopamine is a chemical produced as a reward for some behaviours; these can be positive (e.g. sex, laughter, exercise) and negative (e.g. drug use, aggression). Epinephrine (or adrenaline) is released in times of sudden stress and triggers the fight-or-flight response. Serotonin increases feelings of gratification.

Using Laughology techniques to bring about a humorous response and adapting thinking functions to modulate abnormal mood states will result in a healthier reaction to environmental stressors. This will positively affect temperament and help in rebalancing brain activity and chemical responses.

There is a wealth of medical research from around the world which demonstrates that humour heals. More exciting explorations are taking place in the field of psychoneuroimmunology, which, as explained in Chapter 4, deals with the physiological functioning of the neuro-immune system in states of health and disease. The phrase psychneuroimmunology was first used by Robert Ader (a psychologist) and Nicholas Cohen (an immunologist) in 1975 at the University of Rochester where they studied the psychological impact of stress on the immune system using lab rats.[1] Further studies into the connection between the brain, our emotive state and the immune system support the understanding that a happy and joyful approach to life can promote energy, vitality and health. Scientists are also beginning to discover that the areas of brain activity related to humour have medical benefits. As Norman Cousins realized, watching comedy really does seem to reduce pain and aid healing. More evidence is also coming to light that humour can help to boost the immune system and Cousins even set up a centre for research on the subject.[2]

---

1 See http://www.urmc.rochester.edu/libraries/miner/historical_services/archives/Faculty/PapersofRobertAder.cfm (accessed 31 May 2012).
2 The Cousins Center for Psychoneuroimmunology is based at the University of California, Los Angeles. See http://www.semel.ucla.edu/cousins.

So if we can consciously intercept our thoughts using a humour process before they subconsciously cause a response (as in the diagram below) – which is the basis of CBT – we can then, in certain circumstances, find the humour perspective:

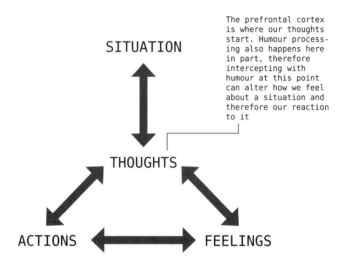

The prefrontal cortex is where our thoughts start. Humour processing also happens here in part, therefore intercepting with humour at this point can alter how we feel about a situation and therefore our reaction to it

To sum up: humour is a cognitive skill that is learnt; and if a skill is learnt it means it can be enhanced. Thoughts create feelings and our feelings cause us to respond and react. If we can intercept negative thoughts with humour, using a developed toolkit based on our understanding of how humour is formed, we can impact on our feelings about the situation and generally act better, make superior choices and choose more proactive behaviours:

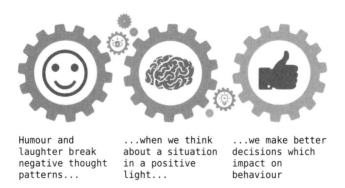

Humour and laughter break negative thought patterns...

...when we think about a situation in a positive light...

...we make better decisions which impact on behaviour

# ACTING UP

The next time you're feeling down, try to identify the thought that is causing this effect and see if you can approach it from another perspective. For example, if you had been thinking, 'I have been dumped again, this always happens to me', try thinking, 'They were not right for me, they would have annoyed me in the long term anyway'. Perhaps you could even try to put a humorous spin on it!

Or try this exercise:

1   Think of a topic that causes you some problems.

2   Write the topic in the middle of a page and create a comedy-gram around it (this is just a spidergram but funnier!). Add observations about the subject that could be viewed as humorous. The key at this stage is not to try too hard to be funny. The thing about observational humour is that it's funny because it's true. Simply highlighting it as an observation that is either stereotypical or quirky gives it a different perspective and can normalise it and thereby help us perceive it as humorous. Here is an example:

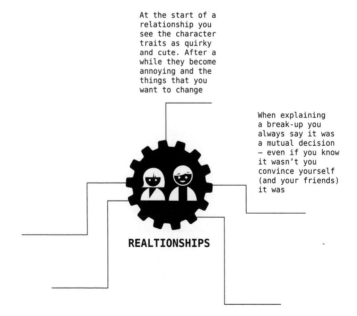

3    In the spaces left have a go at adding your own suggestions.

The point of this exercise is to help improve our humour perspective. One of the most important aspects of the Laughology philosophy is to understand that humour perspective is a personal, internal thinking skill that helps with external responses. This is something *you* need to work at and whilst we recognise that humour perspective can't be learnt overnight, it can be learnt and it starts with you. Ask yourself these questions:

1    What is your perspective on the world? Where has this come from?

2    How do you use humour now and why?

3    Can you really laugh at yourself?

4    What language do you use when talking about situations that have happened and interactions with friends or family?

And so............................................................................

............................................................................

............................................................................

1    Where do you need to challenge your perspective? Use a comedy-gram to do this and help you change the way you see it, using humour to desensitize and review it.

2    In what areas of your life would you like to start using humour more? This is a good starting point for improvements. Would you like to use it in a deflective or reflective way?

3    Think about the last time you reacted negatively. Using a comedy-gram to find a different perspective, could you have reacted differently?

Although I recognise you can't always stop what you are doing to draw a comedy-gram, the more you practise this way of reflecting on events, past and present, the more you will be able to apply this type of thinking. Taking time out of a situation to reflect rather than react immediately can help you do this.

# PART TWO

## LAUGHOLOGY –
## YOUR HUMOUR TOOLKIT

**F**OCUS
**L**ANGUAGE
**I**MAGINATION
**P**ATTERN BREAKING

# PUTTING LAUGHTER AND HUMOUR TO GOOD USE

There are many different ways to use laughter and humour. The unique thing about Laughology is that it can be broken down into simple methods and techniques that can be learned and applied in your own life. Not everyone wants to be a comedian, but humour can offer a way to lift your mood, to see things from a different angle and to be a happier and more resilient human being.

Now you know the practical and scientific basis behind the development of Laughology, the following chapters will give you an easy-to-use and practical guide for how to utilise the humour toolkit in your own life. One of the key methods Laughology emphasises is the ability to change your perspective and subsequently change your emotional state in times of stress – to FLIP your mood and give yourself a clearer view of events unencumbered by negativity.

Here's how to FLIP your mood!

# CHAPTER 9

# YOUR HUMOUR TOOLKIT:
# F IS FOR FOCUS
## L
## I
## P

Have you ever gone to a party that you didn't want to go to and when you got there had to pretend to be enjoying yourself? You might do this by smiling, speaking with a lift in your voice, joking around or trying to look like you are happy. Initially these actions are fake and can feel fake. However, after a while a strange thing happens – you actually begin to enjoy yourself and feel good about the situation. Because you are acting as if you are having a good time, you start to convince yourself that you are actually having a good time! This happens because the motor neurone function of the brain recognises that the actions you are performing – smiling, laughing, being socially engaged – relate to an emotional state, i.e. happiness.

You know how you act when you are in a good mood, so when you are pretending to feel good you focus your behaviour on these actions. Your brain then picks up on the behaviour and recognises it as happiness, and consequently sends out signals that are used to respond to that behaviour.

Even your facial expressions will have an impact on your mood and how others respond to you.

Let's look at this in more detail. Knowing what you can do to affect your mood is important. We all subconsciously act in certain ways when we are happy or sad and these actions support how we feel. By noticing these behaviours you can begin to identify positive and negative traits which support constructive or unconstructive moods and help you to gain control of your frame of mind. Not only can this have a positive effect on your mood but also that of others around you.

These positive behaviours are what we at Laughology call your 'good humour ingredients'. We call them ingredients because it's like baking a cake. If you baked a cake and didn't know what ingredients you'd added then you wouldn't know how to make the same cake again. But if you write down all the ingredients, in the right order, you will be able to repeat the process.

It's the same with knowing what makes us feel good inside. If we *focus* on what these feel-good factors are then we can act them out even if we don't feel like it. Knowing what these behaviours are enables us to act ourselves into a happier state. You could even say the F stands for 'fake it'. (As a fun reminder of the ingredients of humour you could remember it by using the phrase 'fake it, fake it, until you make it!')

Make a note below of all the positive ways you communicate with others when you're talking about something you enjoy or that makes you feel happy. You might want to do this exercise next time you are talking to a friend about a fun activity you have taken part in. Note the way you are telling the story, your facial expressions, the tone and pitch of your voice, your body language, even the types of words you are using. I've added some to start you off.

Smile when you talk

Make eye contact

Open body language

. . . . . . . . . . . . . . . . . . . . . . . . . . . . . . . . . . . . . . . . . . . . . . . . . . . . . . . . . . . . . .

. . . . . . . . . . . . . . . . . . . . . . . . . . . . . . . . . . . . . . . . . . . . . . . . . . . . . . . . . . . . . .

. . . . . . . . . . . . . . . . . . . . . . . . . . . . . . . . . . . . . . . . . . . . . . . . . . . . . . . . . . . . . .

This next exercise aims to help you to understand the connection between behaviours and feelings. Think about the last time you had a good laugh, something/someone who makes you laugh or a place you like to be – any positive thought will do. Describe it to someone else and try to remember your behaviours as you do so. Write down what you notice using the following categories:

| | |
|---|---|
| Facial expressions | |
| Body language | |
| Voice tone | |
| Type of words (i.e. positive language) | |

Over the next week, when something or someone makes you feel good, write it down and think about how you reacted. Reflect on all the things you have done in the week that made you feel good. By the following week you should have a long list of all the things that give you the feel-good factor.

. . . . . . . . . . . . . . . . . . . . . . . . . . . . . . . . . . . . . . . . . . . . . . . . . . . . . . . . . . . . . .

. . . . . . . . . . . . . . . . . . . . . . . . . . . . . . . . . . . . . . . . . . . . . . . . . . . . . . . . . . . . . .

. . . . . . . . . . . . . . . . . . . . . . . . . . . . . . . . . . . . . . . . . . . . . . . . . . . . . . . . . . . . . .

Experiment with behaving in ways that make you and others respond in a positive and happy way. For example, make a conscious effort to smile more at others and notice if people around you smile back at you. If you feel good then you will spread your happiness to others.

The way we communicate with others has a direct bearing on how they perceive us and communicate with us. If your body language is negative it will inevitably elicit an unenthusiastic response. Even if you don't want to converse with someone in a positive way, because you are in a bad mood with them, sometimes it is better to take a step back and think about a more good-natured way of communicating (e.g. using a softer tone of voice or a calmer demeanour). You may not feel like doing this, but if you focus and override your instinctive emotional response, which will be heightened and causing incongruous thoughts, you will inevitably get a better outcome sooner.

For example, I regularly present to small and large audiences about what I do. As someone who talks about laughter, humour and happiness, the way I connect with my audience should be upbeat, positive and happy. It would be rather disappointing if you went to see a speaker talk about laughter and humour and the presentation was dull and the presenter was negative. As I know my personal positive behaviours and communicators well, I know what to focus on to be able to act these out. For me it's about making eye contact so I raise my eyebrows when I talk to help facilitate this. I also smile when I talk, I use tone to get across a positive message, I use my hands to speak and I adopt open body language. I know that presenting in this way will get a positive response from the audience. It can sometimes feel unnatural and difficult and occasionally I have days when I don't feel like being happy and positive; I'm human, after all. However, in these situations I know I have to adopt these affirmative traits in order to get the reaction I need.

It's the same with relationships. We often get stuck in a behavioural rut with others, responding and reacting in ways that have become the norm. We forget how we used to want to make the other person feel and what behaviours from us would elicit that positive response. In any relationship it's important to remember what impact your behaviour is having on how you feel about the person and how they feel about you. If you've got into the habit of being miserable or not doing fun things together any more, you're going to cognitively associate gloomy feelings with that person. So focus on positive behaviours which could change that. Yes, you may have to act it out at first, but after a time it will start to feel natural. Eventually happy emotions will be linked to that person again.

For example, many of us have individuals in our lives who we have challenging relationships with but whom we cannot avoid – these may be work colleagues, family members or even friends (the mood hoovers I mentioned in Chapter 3). It is not always possible or realistic to cut these people out of our lives or ignore them, so we have to find a way of managing the relationship which works for both parties. Sometimes these connections can settle into a pattern of passive acceptance; at other times, one party can take the initiative and develop the relationship into a more meaningful and enriching friendship. In order to do this you have to consciously adopt behaviours that will encourage the other person to feel positive about you. For instance, you may go out of your way to remember details such as their birthday, the name of their pet or enquire about their well-being, even if you don't actually feel like it! But it will pay dividends.

The old adage that you can choose your friends but you can't choose your family is often true. However, it is possible to become closer to family members who you may not see eye to eye with by making efforts like keeping in regular contact and hugging or touching them (appropriately!) during family gatherings. Text messages are also a great way to maintain contact and build a relationship.

A good rule to remember is not to let your feelings get in the way of progress. No one can act happy all the time and we all have arguments and disagreements which can leave us feeling hurt. Nonetheless, we shouldn't let our negative feelings dictate behaviours like sulking, which in turn will keep you stuck in that mode. Instead concentrate on positive actions to get you to the constructive outcome you want: FLIP your behaviour by focusing on the good behaviours that will shift your mood and feeling.

Think about a relationship you have that is negative – this may be with a particular person, with work or even with food. What behaviours do you do that you could change? First, write down how you think about the person/thing and the way you act around them:

........................................................................

........................................................................

........................................................................

Next write down what behaviours you do around the person/thing (we don't refer to them at this point as *negative* behaviours; they are just behaviours that support a feeling):

........................................................................

........................................................................

........................................................................

What behaviours could you do to FLIP your feelings? To help, think of the opposite to the negative behaviours you have identified above. For example, if a relationship with a colleague makes you tense up, sigh or become snappy, the opposite reaction will be smiling when you talk to them and making a conscious effort to adopt open body language (e.g. positive touches on the arm, if appropriate, when speaking to them). If disagreements with this person make you irritable and argumentative, think of its converse. Instead you might say: 'I see your point' and leave it at that. We will address language and communication further in the next section. Write down opposing behaviours to counteract the negative list above:

........................................................................

........................................................................

........................................................................

What response would you like to see from this? What reaction do you think you would get? (Really think this through so you know how your behaviours could play out.)

.....................................................................

.....................................................................

.....................................................................

Being aware of your behaviour in the first instance will help you realise how you can impact on your and other people's feelings. It may be that for now you just monitor how you respond in certain situations. Then start thinking about how you can counteract this by flipping your behaviour and acting more positively. This will eventually lead to you feeling better, getting a more positive response from others and building happier relationships.

Knowing what you do when you are upbeat and happy is vital to shifting your mood and feeling better, but it is also important to recognise what you do when you feel down and sad. You will have behaviours that support your negative feelings too; being aware of what you do in these situations and being able to FLIP this and focus on behaviours that are more conducive to you feeling better will move you forward and out of a negative situation quicker.

Think about what happens to our body when we're stressed: we breathe quicker and our heart races. We can learn to manage this by controlling our breathing, calming the mind with distracting thoughts and using our laughter triggers. What other activities calm you if you're feeling anxious or nervous? Once you are aware what these are you can focus on them when you need to FLIP your mood. Write these down here:

.....................................................................

.....................................................................

.....................................................................

Awareness of these strategies can help in situations when our thoughts are overtaken by negative feelings and we need to focus on behaviours that will help to adjust our mood.

# POINTS TO REMEMBER

- Feeling happy and positive in yourself will impact on your behaviour towards others.

- Know what makes you happy – keep a list of your positive behaviours.

- We are social beings so having a positive group of people to interact with can help lift our mood.

- Change doesn't happen overnight; at first it will feel unusual and uncomfortable to do something different, but stick with it and it will become natural.

CHAPTER 10

# YOUR HUMOUR TOOLKIT:

F

## L IS FOR LANGUAGE

I

P

Be careful of your thoughts; they may become
words at any moment.

Ira Gassen

In the previous chapter you were asked to think about a situation that
made you feel good and how you could use this to help yourself act
differently and feel better. Language can be used in much the same
way. This chapter focuses on language and how this can affect our
mood.

The spoken word has incredible power, be that words you say out
loud or the words you say in your head – your internal dialogue.
Language can help to change the way you feel and enable you to
reframe a situation. Every day the brain makes tiny adaptations to our
environment. This constant adjustment is called *neuroplasticity*. Our
brains change and adapt in response to stimuli and create new neural
pathways and connections. In some cases the process of neuroplasticity enables injured brains to repair themselves by rerouting damaged
neural pathways, which allows the subject to relearn functions previously lost. With repetitive practice some stroke victims can learn to
reuse an affected limb because other parts of the brain begin to take
over the movement function for that limb.

Neuroplasticity is the physical process of the brain rewiring itself, and language is one of the tools it uses to do this. Language helps us to frame our beliefs and feelings about a situation. We use words to describe and make sense of the world and our feelings; therefore by modifying our language we can adjust our perspective and communicate differently with others.

For example, if you constantly tell yourself that something is hard to do you will build a belief around that task which reinforces the idea that it is difficult or impossible. However, the link between the task and your belief that it is hard is created by neuroplasticity. By the same process, if you use different language – for instance, substituting the word 'hard' for the word 'challenging', which we understand to mean achievable – our brains will reframe how we view that task and subsequently we will perceive it more positively.

An adaptable brain allows us to make positive changes. When used in a constructive way this can have a profound impact on our experiences and frame of mind. Conversely, if you are repetitively thinking and verbalising negative thoughts, you are actually strengthening the neural pathways in your brain that support continued negative thinking. Words express feelings and reinforce the brain to remain in that unhelpful thought pattern. If your speech is filled with fearful comments, self-condemnation, dismissive remarks about others, complaints or self-pity, you are literally talking yourself into more of the same.

As mentioned in previous chapters, you can choose to focus your mind on positive and affirming thoughts and behaviours, even if you don't feel happy or positive at that moment, and by doing so you will stimulate and reinforce the 'happy' part of your brain. With repetitive practice your feelings will change for the better, supported by a stronger, happier brain function.

To help accelerate the process of feeling positive and happy, and even to create more laughter and fun in your life, you can change your language to reflect your positive thinking. Words put action behind thought and give it momentum and reality. *Awareness of your own thought and language habits is the key to this work.*

Think for a minute about a positive experience you have had and write down all the words you associate with that event:

..........................................................................

..........................................................................

..........................................................................

Now think of something you don't like doing and write down some of the words you associate with this activity:

..........................................................................

..........................................................................

..........................................................................

Talking and using words in a positive way is called 'solution-focused language' because a lot of what we say comes from our feelings. Communication is not only about *what* we say but *how* we say it. We 'talk' with our whole body and other people pick up on these messages and respond in a similar way. If we can use affirmative, solution-focused language we are more likely to get a more positive reaction, which will in turn make us feel better.

For example, rather than telling a child 'Don't drop the cup!', say 'Hold onto the cup – be careful!', which is more action and solution-focused. There are negative actions in the first sentence ('drop the cup') which we register more keenly than 'don't'. We can use positive language to get to where we, and others, want to be.

Solution-focused and positive language isn't just about external dialogue; it has a lot to do with internal discourse too. For example, rather than just thinking 'I'm having a really bad day', it would be more productive to assert, 'I'll feel better when I can get to the bottom of this paperwork'.

Remember to use the golden three-step rule:

1   Share the problem.

2   Find the solution.

3   Move forward – don't get stuck going over the problem.

Let's try an example:

1   I feel like I've got a cold coming on. I'm feeling bored and a bit down in the dumps and don't feel like doing anything.

2   But I'll feel better if I go and visit my friend, John.

3   He always cheers me up!

Or alternatively:

1   I feel like I've got a cold coming on. I'm feeling bored and a bit down in the dumps and don't feel like doing anything.

2   I'll take a nice hot bath, have some lemon and honey and go to bed early.

3   Tomorrow I'll feel much better and be able to get on with life.

Although it is good to talk and share a problem, because a problem shared is a problem halved, it is important not to dwell on difficulties and make them the focus of your thinking.

Language can also diffuse negative situations. Let's take an example from my own life. As a stand-up I spend many hours in green rooms with other comedians. The choice of language among comics can be a little blue at times and I got into the habit of swearing and using bad language. Also as a comedian you end up spending many hours in the car on motorways. This can be intense and I would often get a little road rage if I was in a situation where another driver did something I perceived as wrong. I would swear at the car/person and feel my rage and stress levels increasing. If the driver saw me it would cause an even worse response. So I began practising using inoffensive and silly phrases when this happened – simple things like 'Whoopsie daisy!' or 'Silly monkey!' As they are innocuous and daft, I found that I didn't get angry and thereby became a much less stressed driver, which was a good result for everyone.

It is relatively easy to substitute unhelpful words for more helpful ones. Rather than saying 'I'm worried about my driving test', you could say 'My driving test is coming up – it's going to be a challenge but I'm looking forward to having the freedom to drive by myself'. Or 'I can't do maths – it's too hard' could become 'I might need extra help with maths'.

I remember the first long flight I took on my own for work. I was going to Israel and had a stopover in Prague. I was quite nervous, especially as I had to change planes in an airport where English was not the main language. As I got on the airplane my phone rang – it was my dad calling to ask how I was feeling and whether I was excited. 'You'll be great, enjoy it and see it as a new adventure,' he told me. After that my mindset changed – his positive words had reframed my feelings. Pay attention to your thoughts and words all the time and commit to proactively speaking positively about situations and people. Practise words of appreciation at least three times a day and regularly remove yourself from negative conversations. *Words are tools that can set you free and change your life. Choose them wisely.*

We have all reacted in a destructive or argumentative way using language and wondered later why we said what we did in the way we did and wished we had responded differently. Negative responses usually cause a bad reaction in others. Thinking carefully about what we want to say before we say it can be the difference between a trivial issue being blown out of proportion or being dealt with in a more sensible way. Just because you believe negative language is being used towards you does not mean you should respond in kind. Your positive language can help you to find a solution.

Think of a situation where you wish you had reacted differently. What was said to you and how did you reply? What words did you use to say something different from what you felt inside? Why do you think you used negative words? Was it because you were hurt, angry or upset? If so, what would have been a better way of expressing this in a calm and solution-focused manner? Use this as an example to consider how you might use solution-focused and positive language to FLIP a similar situation in the future.

OK, now think of a situation where you were told something that made you feel great. What kind of words were used – friendly, complimentary, soothing, assenting? How did the person talking to you use their voice? Was it slow and calm or fast and excited? High or low pitch? Heavy or light rhythm? Loud or quiet? Comparing the two experiences and the types of language used will help you think about how language and the way we use it can have an impact on the way we think and feel about a situation and how people react and respond to us.

The words you use and how you say them affect how others respond to you. If they are angry, you can calm them down. If they are sad, you can cheer them up. Words also affect how you feel about yourself. If you are sad, think about how you could use positive language to lift your mood. If you are angry, think calming thoughts using language to help yourself relax. For comedians language is very important to engage or disengage an audience. The old adage 'it's all in the delivery' is very true, not just in comedy but in everyday life. To quote the great philosophers Bananarama: 'It aint what you do, it's the way that you do it.' Comedians are brilliant wordsmiths and choose their words very carefully to create a comical meaning to otherwise normal discretions. The language we choose and how we present an idea will have a huge impact on the way we feel, how we perceive things and how others feel and make sense of a situation. For example, you could say to a child 'Just try the food, you might like it! (the two words here 'try' and 'might' suggest a negative feeling may also be in play). Changing the sentence to 'It's really scrumptious stuff, just put an incy wincy bit on your fork to taste' makes use of playful language.

If you don't like something, and you constantly tell yourself you don't like it, the language will support how you feel about it. Perhaps change the don't like for 'challenge' or 'face up to' which suggests bravery instead.

Words that are fun, motivating and positive can help you feel better and encourage others think about a situation in a different light. Try thinking of some phrases you use and see if you can change the language to make them sound more solution-focused. Here are a few examples:

| Phrase | Negative connotation | Consider using |
|---|---|---|
| Yes but … | The *but* discounts the *yes* | Yes and have you also considered....... ..................................... ..................................... . If you mean no say no! |
| What do you expect me to do about it? | I don't want to know and I'm not interested in helping | It sounds a bit bonkers at the moment I need to get my head around it |

Have a go at writing down words or phrases that make you laugh or feel good or inspire opportunity. Being aware of these and using them in everyday life will make a difference in your delivery and response. Some examples are: possibility, fruity, aroused, orifice (I often substitute this for office and invite people to meet me in my orifice – which definitely gets a positive response!). Have a go below:

.............................................................................

.............................................................................

.............................................................................

Now think about how you might use this language in everyday life to help you and others feel better, bring about a smile and maybe even a laugh.

Language is powerful for desensitising information and can make the difference between feeling good or bad about something. In comedy wordplay is essential for creating a twist or the joke. Comedians use double entendres, puns, similes and much more to send up a situation and talk about taboo subjects. Clever use of language can break down social barriers and allow new lines of communication to open.

One of my favourite examples of this is Lee Mack talking about his granddad going into a home; an event many of us can associate with:

```
It was very sad when my granddad went into
this home, it was very sad …  it wasn't his
home. No really, he went into this home and I
rang grandma one day to ask how he was getting
on. She said 'Oh, he's like a fish out of
water.' 'Oh,' I said, 'is he finding it hard
to adjust?' 'No,' she said, 'he's dead.'
```

Later on in the routine he refers to finding 'wacky backy' under his grandma's bed – then goes on to say it wasn't the drug, it was the Sri Lankan wicket-keeper.

Mack uses language brilliantly here to introduce sensitive topics, such as older family members dying and FLIPs them on their head. Also using the term 'wacky backy' is a great example of how language can amplify a comical situation. It is a funny phrase in itself – far funnier than marijuana or cannabis – and therefore adds to the hilarity of the anecdote.

Some words are just funny and you can use these as well as your laughter triggers as comedy word triggers. Think of all the words that make you laugh or bring a smile to your face. Write them here:

.........................................................................

.........................................................................

.........................................................................

If you need to, how can you sneak these words into your everyday life to help you laugh, feel better and reframe a situation?

# TOP TIPS

- **Start your day with positive language.** When you wake up, tell yourself what kind of day you are going to have. For example, 'I intend to have a fun, happy and productive day'. Even if you know you have a hard day ahead, don't say to yourself that it's going to be hard. Instead say, 'I have a challenging but exciting day ahead and will use all my positive skills to deal with it successfully'.

- **Use positive self-talk.** Using positive talk and language about yourself or rehearsing a conversation, presentation or situation in your mind can really help when it comes to the real thing. This verbal activity will reinforce the feelings behind your words. Talking out loud to yourself helps the brain connect the words with the activity. For example, if you have been feeling nervous about an event or task, tell yourself you can do it and that you feel relaxed and calm. This will really help in the situation.

- **Thoughts are internalised language.** Pay attention to your thoughts; if you catch yourself in a negative thought pattern, break it by saying something that is completely opposite. Challenge unconstructive thoughts with a positive phrase or a funny word or saying. How can you use language to reframe a thought, desensitise it and assign a different meaning to it?

- **Communicate thanks.** Take time to look around you and acknowledge with others what you are grateful for. We are surrounded by goodness, beauty and humour. If we take the time to see them and articulate them, we begin to feel and see them more.

- **Don't get sucked in to negative conversations.** When individuals start being mean about others or downbeat about their day, excuse yourself from the conversation. If that's not possible, use your own skills to be a positive influence in the exchange and don't get drawn in to participating in the negative chatter.

■ **Use solution-focused language to talk yourself through difficulties.** From time to time you will speak about negative or painful experiences. This is not a bad thing and can help us to let go of unpleasant feelings and memories. It can be a necessary part of the healing process. However, follow up the negative words with positive words and actions. Speak about hoping to feel better and moving forward. This will help you start to feel that there is a route to getting better.

■ **Use words to empower or desensitise.** Choose the words you use internally and externally carefully. Words are powerful and can be triggers to laughter and humour. How can you use them to help you and others feel better?

```
Keep my words positive. Words become my
behaviours. Keep my behaviours positive.
Behaviours become my habits. Keep my habits
positive, because my habits become my values.
Keep my values positive, because my values
become my destiny. There is no dress
rehearsal. This is one day in our life.
                                       Gandhi
```

Over the next week write in your work pages the times you use language to FLIP your mood. The more you use FLIP to alter your mood, the easier it gets. Concentrating on positive, solution-focused language will make you feel good. Choosing your words carefully to get a message across and to engage others can be the key to opening a door or closing one. Use positive language with others and observe the encouraging response you get!

# CHAPTER 11

# YOUR HUMOUR TOOLKIT:

F
L
# I IS FOR IMAGINATION
P

In the previous chapter I asked you to think about the language you used in a situation when you had to act differently from how you actually felt. Now I want you to use your *imagination* to help you feel better, happier and more positive, which in turn will help you find solutions to life's ups and downs.

Your imagination can work for you and against you. The trick is to understand how the positive and negative aspects of imagination affect our feelings and behaviour. For example, have you ever been looking forward to something so much that you get butterflies of excitement? Can you remember what that was? Use your imagination to take you back there and write down everything that's happening in your body right now.

.............................................................................

.............................................................................

.............................................................................

That's just your imagination. It is powerful enough to have a physical impact on your body. However, this can also function in unpleasant ways. When you remember past situations or think about an event that is going to happen in the future you might become physically anxious. You might feel worried, sick and scared which in turn can cause related behavioural responses. For example, have you ever worried about an event and, before you've even got there, your imagination has started to work overtime to the point where you create a terrible story in your head of what is going to happen? You may even talked yourself out of going. Or maybe you've dreamt about having an argument with someone and woken up feeling in a bad mood with them? But it's just your imagination, it's not real. Imagination can work positively in dreams too: we've all had erotic dreams that cause a physical reaction. If you're lucky enough to wake up next to the person in your dream they will most likely get the full benefit of that positivity!

Imagination is not just a subconscious act – you can take control of it and harness it to constructively think through situations or challenges in a different light. Optimistic thinking is just using your imagination to conjure up words and images that are conducive to progression and success. Your imagination is limitless so anything is possible. You can be in a real-life situation that appears serious, humourless and negative, but because your imagination is so powerful you can puncture the seriousness of it with humour. A good example of this is the tried and tested technique used by nervous public speakers who imagine their audiences naked while delivering their speeches. A positive mind anticipates happiness, joy and a successful outcome. If you think in this way you're more likely to work through difficult circumstances positively. Imagination can even be used to diffuse feelings of anger or upset.

Do you remember your laughter triggers from Chapter 2? You can use these to help divert destructive thinking patterns and create joy and laughter in times of stress. This isn't always as easy as just recalling them. Often, if your emotive state is heightened, it is better to momentarily distance yourself from the situation by removing yourself from it either physically by walking away, or mentally by taking deep breaths and counting to ten. This gives you the space to use your imagination and call on your laughter triggers. It may help to write them down or refer to them if you've already done so.

You can also work through a worrying event by using your imagination to reframe the situation by constructing a humorous story around it. Try it. Think of a situation that concerns you and write down your anxieties about it. How might it end?

..........................................................................

..........................................................................

..........................................................................

Now use your imagination and sense of humour to create a different and more productive outcome.

..........................................................................

..........................................................................

..........................................................................

Now keep replaying that alternative scenario in your imagination.

Once you've done this a few times your brain will start to think about the situation in a new light, thereby changing the way you feel about it. Now you feel differently about it, consider how you would ideally like the situation to work out?

..........................................................................

..........................................................................

..........................................................................

Humour is the most useful tool in your bag of tricks when it comes to playing out new thoughts. This process of changing the way you think about events is known as a *paradigm shift*. It enables the change to be non-threatening and can help to instantly alter your perception. Humour creates a channel for the new perception to be captured and realised simultaneously. It enables you to see the absurdity of your thoughts and behaviour without negative judgement. Often, humour can make you aware that you are over-analysing a situation and help put it into perspective.

Positive and negative thinking are both contagious and can impact on other people. This happens instinctively and at a subconscious level – it is transferred through body language, communication and energy. Is it any wonder that we want to be around happy people and avoid miserable ones? So help yourself: be positive by thinking positive and you will find that other people like this are attracted to you more. Negative thoughts, words and attitudes engender negative and unhappy moods and actions. Pessimism can lead to a release of stress hormones, such as cortisol, which in turn cause more unhappiness and negativity.

# TOP TIPS

■ **Always use your imagination constructively and to your benefit.** It doesn't matter what your circumstances are at the present moment. It may take some time for the changes to take place but if you think positively, eventually they will.

■ **Use positive words in your inner dialogues and when talking with others.** If your imagination does start to run wild in a negative way, recognise that this is only your imagination. Stop, take hold of it, tell yourself you *are* in control and think of at least three different outcomes using your imagination which are positive and even fun. Smile a little more, as this also helps us to think positively.

■ **Be aware that negative thoughts can be persistent.** They will try to enter your mind, and the process of replacing them with positive ones is best done through repetition until eventually humour, optimism and positivity become your default position. Sooner or later persistence will teach your mind to think positively and ignore negative thoughts.

You can also use the following exercises to help you when you need to feel positive:

■ Think about the nicest place you've ever seen, whether that is somewhere you've actually visited or a destination you've seen on a photograph, postcard, on TV or in a film. If you can imagine it, you can go there!

■ Write down your favourite places – perhaps your home, a holiday destination, the seaside, quiet woods or a noisy fairground – and imagine them in vivid detail.

....................................................................

....................................................................

....................................................................

■ Think about a funny time. I can guarantee your imagination will help you get there and even make you laugh again!

Keep practising these exercises and they will become easy to do. They will help you to feel better when you are next in a negative place.

Over the next week write down in your work pages how often you FLIP your mood. The more you use FLIP to alter your mood, the easier it gets. Pretty soon you'll be thinking more often of the places that make you feel good and the things that make you laugh, and this will put a smile on your face and give you a lift. Once you feel better you can deal with any challenging situations more productively and think through outcomes in a more positive and proactive way.

# CHAPTER 12

#  YOUR HUMOUR TOOLKIT:
F
L
I
# P IS FOR PATTERN BREAKING

In the previous chapter I asked you to use your imagination in a situation where you had to act differently from how you felt inside. Now I want you to think about breaking *patterns* of behaviour you may be subconsciously hooked into that lead to negative actions and thoughts. This type of pattern breaking encompasses the entire FLIP model.

We often go through life repeating ways of acting and communicating without thinking. We operate predominantly at a subconscious level – picking up habitual behaviours from those around us, learning how to achieve things for ourselves and generally making our way in the world. Some patterns are productive and help us or enrich us. For example, we usually greet a loved one with a smile, a hug and a kiss, and don't necessarily think consciously about doing it; it's just automatic. Other patterns, such as always arguing with someone or generally just poor communication, may not be so advantageous. As discussed in Chapter 3, this can happen through learnt styles of behaviour.

The key to breaking this behaviour is to be aware of the negative patterns you are repeating in your life. For example, it may be that you always become involved in relationships with a certain type of person – the 'bad boy/girl'. Or you may feel that in every job you do you are always being treated unfairly. There may also be positive patterns: you may notice that every time you go out you seem to get bought a drink or you always succeed in interviews.

Can you think of any positive patterns in your life that keep occurring? Write them here:

.........................................................................

.........................................................................

.........................................................................

From your list pick one of these patterns and use the FLIP model to analyse it. For example: what is the behaviour you *focus* on? I'm sure you do this subconsciously. You've learnt to do it over time and it has become habitual because it leads to a positive outcome for you. Now look at the *language* you use in this situation: what positive words or phrases do you use? Now use your *imagination*: how do you think about the situation before you get to it and while you're in it? This will all impact on how you feel – and we know feelings are picked up in our behaviour and passed on to others. With FLIP you can begin to understand why these patterns achieve positive outcomes and create good humour in ourselves and others.

Now let's repeat this exercise but focusing on a recurring pattern that you are not so happy about (e.g. poor communication with a relative, the way you are treated at work). Write this here:

.........................................................................

.........................................................................

.........................................................................

Repeat the FLIP process as described above. Be really honest with yourself about your behaviours, your language and the way you think. What feelings are these creating for you about the situation?

Next comes the tricky part. For something to change you have to recognise where the change will come from – and that change has to come from you. We are not always in control of circumstances and we cannot dictate other people's behaviour, but we can control the way *we* are. Some time ago I came across a great phrase which is a hard but very effective pill to swallow: 'If I am the problem, I am also the solution.' Recognise this simple truth and you will become empowered to change many situations in life.

Back to the exercise: look again at your unhelpful pattern. Can you see a way to unpick the situation and focus on more positive behaviour, language and thought patterns to get a better outcome? Write down your strategy for how you are going to break this pattern and behave differently in the future:

.....................................................................................

.....................................................................................

.....................................................................................

When you are in a bad mood you can alter the way you feel by physically doing something different, thereby breaking the pattern and distracting yourself with your behaviour. Think of some examples of what you have done in the past to change your mood. These might include making a cup of tea or coffee, going for a walk or a bike ride, going to the gym, or taking a shower or a long soak in the bath. Write down as many as you can think of:

.....................................................................................

.....................................................................................

.....................................................................................

Making a conscious decision to distract yourself from an unpleasant mood can help you gain perspective on the causes of these feelings. Looking at the situation from a different point of view can help to shift a disagreeable frame of mind and put things in their proper order. Breaking a pattern, whether it be cognitive or behavioural, is difficult but with awareness and practice it can be done effectively, offering you the opportunity to be proactive rather than reactive.

Comedians learn to break the subconscious patterns of thinking a certain way about a situation and the connection this can have to an emotive state. They take an everyday occurrence – a socially taboo subject, an embarrassing situation or something that could be perceived as upsetting – and change their focus to find a different way of looking at the situation. They use carefully selected language to communicate this to others and to desensitise the situation internally and externally. Their imagination helps them to process the information in a humorous and creative way. This process breaks a pattern of thinking that could otherwise be deemed as taboo or unsettling and normalises it. It makes it funny and easier to digest and, subsequently, in some cases, can make it easier to talk about. Changing the humour perspective of a situation or event can help people affected by it feel better and move forward. Pattern breaking is about recognising behaviours, language and thinking that can leave you stuck in a negative cycle. If you recognise patterns that occur regularly, or feelings that are common to similar situations, there will be something you are doing that is sustaining that emotion. However, the great thing is we are in control of breaking that pattern and being able to FLIP this situation or feeling on its head, allowing us to feel, think and act better.

The comedian Adam Hills does this brilliantly. Adam was born without a right foot and wears a prosthesis. He uses this fact, and people's reactions to it, as subject matter for some of his comedy material. One of my favourite examples is when he described how, when he was at a party explaining to guest that he wore an artificial limb she asked: 'Can you still have sex?' To which Adam replied, 'Yeh! What does your boyfriend do? Does he have a run- up?'

In this instance Adam does two things: he introduces the idea that talking and asking questions about prosthetic limbs is OK. He also normalises the things we may all think, but not necessarily say, about people with artificial limbs and answers some of the questions.

As stated earlier, using humour to change our perspective can be a very personal strategy to help us move forward. It's this personalisation that needs to be taken into account. If it's appropriate for an individual to think and communicate in this way about a personal situation to help them feel better, this can be OK. When using humour outwardly, sensitivity is paramount.

# PART THREE

# FIVE STEPS OF SMILE

# CHAPTER 13

 # THE POWER OF A SMILE

Smiling is a universal language – it is one of the few facial expressions that is understood across all cultures and languages, and could be older than mankind. Professor Jan van Hooff, a well-known expert of emotional facial expressions in primates, argued that the bare-teeth display of chimpanzees is homologous to the human smile.[1] But you don't have to delve into scientific tomes to find proof of the universal nature of the smile – you just have to watch children playing.

A friend of mine had taken her 5-year-old daughter on holiday to Spain. It was the first time the youngster had been abroad and, like most kids on vacation, she found a friend to play with on the beach. She set about building sandcastles and paddling with her new pal.

After an hour or so it was time for lunch and my friend called her daughter back.

'What is your friend's name?' her mum asked.

'I don't know,' replied the little girl, 'she doesn't talk like I do.'

Puzzled, my friend asked how they had managed to understand each other, to which her daughter answered: 'She had the same laugh and the same smile as me.'

A natural smile usually begins with our senses. We see, hear, smell or taste something and the emotional data is channelled to the brain

---

1   J. van Hooff, 'A comparative approach to the phylogeny of laughter and smiling', in R. A. Hinde (ed.), *Non-Verbal Communication* (Cambridge: Cambridge University Press, 1972), pp. 209–240.

where it is interpreted and manifests in a facial expression. Smiles are created by two muscles: the zygomatic major in the cheek which contracts and pulls the lips upward, and the orbicularis oculi which encircles the eye socket and squeezes the outside corners (creating crow's feet!). Other muscles can stimulate a smile, but only these two together produce what is recognised as a genuine expression of positive emotion. Psychologists call this the 'Duchenne smile', named after French anatomist Guillaume Duchenne, who studied facial expressions by stimulating various muscles in the face with electrical currents.

Smiling is something simple we can all do to help ourselves and others. Just the action of smiling helps us feel better. In psychology the theory of facial feedback postulates that 'involuntary facial movements provide sufficient peripheral information to drive emotional experience';[2] in other words the act of smiling in itself elicits emotions. In simple terms, you can improve your mood by smiling. A number of research projects support this hypothesis. Studies have also shown that when you mimic someone else's facial expressions it may cause you to feel empathy for the other person. As Marianne LaFrance, author of *Lip Service: Smiles in Life, Death, Trust, Lies, Work, Memory, Sex, and Politics* says: 'Smiles are universally recognized and understood for what they show and convey, yet not necessarily for what they *do*. Smiles are much more than cheerful expressions. They are social acts with consequences.'[3] When you smile, the world really does appear better.

Laughter and smiles are not always appropriate in depressing situations but research does prove that smiling helps people in difficult circumstances – the reason why gallows humour is so commonly displayed by those employed in challenging vocations. In a study by Dacher Keltner and George Bonanno of the Catholic University, the facial expressions of people were recorded when they discussed a recently deceased spouse.[4] The researchers found lower levels of dis-

2   D. A. Bernstein, A. Clarke-Stewart, L. A. Penner, E. J. Roy and C. D. Wickens, *Psychology, 5th edn.* (Boston, MA: Houghton Mifflin, 2000).

3   M. LaFrance, *Lip Service: Smiles in Life, Death, Trust, Lies, Work, Memory, Sex, and Politics* (New York: W.W. Norton, 2011).

4   D. Keltner and G. A. Bonanno, 'A study of laughter and dissociation: the distinct correlates of laughter and smiling during bereavement', *Journal of Personality and Social Psychology* 73 (1997), 687–702.

tress in those who displayed genuine Duchenne smiles during the discussion compared to those who did not.

The benefits of smiling through grief appear to occur on a biological level as well. Barbara Fredrickson and Robert Levenson observed the facial expressions made by 72 people watching a funeral scene from the film *Steel Magnolias*.[5] The 50 participants who smiled at least once during the clip recovered their baseline cardiovascular levels more quickly than others who failed to smile.

Not only do people deduce useful information from smiles, they also use this knowledge to direct their own behaviour. In an experiment, researchers found that people showed a greater preference for working with individuals displaying genuine Duchenne smiles than those bearing false smiles.[6]

The ability to draw on a genuine smile, using tried and tested laughter triggers, is thus a skill that will not only make you feel good but will benefit those around you. In many cultures smiling is highly valued. Buddhists use the act of smiling to bring about a feeling of peace and serenity. As Zen master and famed peace activist Thich Nhat Hanh says: 'Sometimes your joy is the source of your smile, but sometimes your smile can be the source of your joy.'

Laughology uses an acronym which can help us to live a happier life every day if we stick to these five simple SMILE rules:

1   **Smile.** Take active steps to be aware of how frequently you smile. Note how many times you smile each day and try to increase this by 10%. When you start to smile more, be aware of the changes in the way you feel and in the way others react to you. At first you may feel like a fake, but as I've explained, we are primed to recognise genuine smiles so if you use your laughter triggers to bring about a smile it will be genuine. It may feel odd at first – smiling is learnt behaviour and you may have grown up in a household where there was not much laughter or smiling – but practice makes perfect. Smiling is a natural act so

---

5   J. J. Gross, B. L. Fredrickson and R. W. Levenson, 'The psychophysiology of crying', *Psychophysiology* 31 (1994), 460–468.

6   M. J. Bernstein, D. F. Sacco, C. M. Brown, S. G. Young and H. M. Claypool, 'A preference for genuine smiles following social exclusion', *Journal of Experimental Social Psychology* 46 (2010), 196–199.

you will soon feel comfortable. If you are about to make a tricky phone call, smile before you dial. If you are about to go into an awkward situation, stop and smile before you walk through the door. Use your smile as a primer to switch on positivity.

2   **Moment of magic.** Look for opportunities to do good for other people and create a moment of magic in someone else's life. Acting selflessly results in lots of positive emotions. This isn't just anecdotal – research has shown that activity in the reward centre of the brain increases when you do something altruistic.[7] Sadly we get so busy and caught up in our own lives that we often let opportunities to help others pass us by; and by ignoring them we pass up the opportunity to enrich our own lives. A moment of magic can be anything from helping an elderly person to cross the road to assisting someone who looks lost. Start to look around you for people who may need some help: does that man at the train station need directions? Does that old lady need a hand with her shopping? Opportunities to assist others are usually fleeting so act on them quickly; don't stop to analyse the situation. Helping people and carrying out kind acts helps you understand more about yourself and what makes you happy. It also enables you to have a better perspective on your own advantages and appreciate how lucky you are. If all you think about is yourself, all you will understand is yourself. Just one act of kindness will elicit a smile from another person and their smile may transfer to someone else too. What a brilliant chain reaction.

3   **Impulse.** Act on your positive impulses. Modern life is not conducive to impulsive action; thanks in part to technology we delegate many decisions in our lives and are led in the choices we make. For example, typing in a destination on a sat nav will give you the most efficient route but it may not give you the most interesting one. Whenever you use a search engine the results you get back are based on what the software thinks you prefer based on your past patterns of use. Shopping has become less impulsive as supermarkets record our buying patterns and use them to inform our future choices. Even dating and finding

7   D. Tankersley, C. J. Stowe, and S. A Huettel, 'Altruism is associated with an increased neural response to agency', *Nature Neuroscience* 10 (2007), 150–151.

your ideal partner has been outsourced to computer programmes which are designed to match you with personality types similar to your own. While all these advances are helpful, they take away opportunities for us to act spontaneously and use our instincts and intuition. It is often impulsive behaviour that shifts our lives in new and interesting directions – and it adds variety, which we all know is the spice of life. Generally people tend to stagnate – they analyse and act on reason. But if you have a positive thought it is generally a good one. Don't try to unpick it and add negatives, just do it. If you stop and think too much, you will find you are forever talking yourself out of things. Get involved!

4    **Laughter.** Think about where you can create more laughter in your life and the lives of people around you. What do you do in your family and in your relationships that brings about laughter? Try to increase these activities and work out how you can create more of them. Keep a laughter diary for a week and review it daily. Write down how many times you laugh during the day and what makes you laugh. If at the end of the day you feel as though there has not been enough laughter in your life, use your laughter triggers the following day to create more.

5    **Empower.** Empower yourself in a positive way. Use Laughology to help yourself, and others, to boost levels of happiness, confidence and well-being. Give yourself permission to dictate your mood and how you see the world. How you cope with the stresses and strains that life inevitably throws at you will define how you move forward and the way you feel about life in general. Use laughter and humour to bring about the positive changes you want to see in your life. Take control of your own happiness – don't wait for other people to make you happy or sit around waiting for things to change. People stuck in a rut often look to some future event, such as a holiday or a change in circumstance, and pin their hopes on this to create happiness. How many times have you heard (or said), 'I'll feel better when …'? Rather than wait, empower yourself and act now to feel better. I have often heard people saying 'I want to empower you'. My belief is you are not given empowerment, you take it!

# EPILOGUE

The last 45 years or so have seen an increase in rules, regulations and working practices that are measured and quantified. This represents decades in schools and workplaces that are system-led, rule-led and target-led. Clearly we need standards and yardsticks, but are we forgetting that the essence of evolution is change? For change to happen we need to go beyond the norm; we need ideas and imagination – and these come from play.

By measuring and systemising everything we are quashing personal expression, individuality, creativity and innovation, which are at the epicentre of advancement in everything from organisations to government agendas. Instead we have become institutionalised to think, act and behave in a certain way. The consensus seems to be that real work can only be done when we get serious. So my plea to you is to get playing, be creative, have fun and laugh!

The propensity towards seriousness at the expense of creativity and diversity sets in early. Our education system is partly responsible; it has done little to change over the years and retains a didactic style of teaching by rote. Creative, enthusiastic teachers are the exception and are in need. In nursery and infant school we are encouraged to play, laugh, have fun and explore. But at secondary school we are told how to learn, that questions have specific answers and that tasks are performed in a systemised way. We learn best when we play – it is how we discover the world and its meaning to us as individuals; but clearly this is going to be very different for everyone.

If you ask people what they want for their children, the reply is often for them to grow into independent, happy, positive, self-motivated (and lots of other positive words that describe someone's outlook) people. Of course you want them to be successful and be comfortable, but how do we measure success and what dictates comfort? I have come across many individuals who are materially comfortable; they have what they want in terms of material things. However, when it comes to the deeper meaning of the word – ease of body and mind, feeling relaxed and free of anxiety – quite often these are far from being attained. In fact, if you scratch the surface, you get a feeling of complete discomfort. We need to readdress the balance between material comforts and understand the real sense of the word – and, yes, it is all about balance and expectation.

The one fact we need to remember is that we are never going to be happy all the time. Life throws up challenges and difficulties on a daily basis and the trick is not to ignore or walk away from these but to face them head on with the right tools and attitude. Facing dilemmas in your life and getting through them is in part what makes us who we are – it builds our character and enables us to learn from mistakes. Without sadness you can't have happiness; the two go hand in hand like yin and yang. This ancient Chinese philosophy of complementary forces helps us to meet the difficult times with positivity and the knowledge that we will get through them.

This book is very much about finding perspective on life. Some problems are bigger than others and some are not worth spending time worrying about. As theologian Reinhold Niebuhr says in his Serenity Prayer: 'God, grant me the serenity to accept the things I cannot change, the courage to change the things I can, and the wisdom to know the difference.' Or, as I say, don't sweat the small stuff.

People often presume I am always laughing and smiling. Much of the time I am, but of course I'm not continually ecstatic – it would be exhausting! There are plenty of times when I feel miserable or I just fancy having a strop; it is in our nature and completely natural to be sad sometimes. Laughology doesn't set out to make you perpetually happy, nor is it a recipe for a perfect way of living; in life perfection is incredibly illusive. What Laughology does is to help you find ways to make your life happier and, more importantly, it gives you the tools to face those difficult times with resilience. If used regularly, the techniques I have outlined in this book will allow you to step back from the brink in times of trouble and re-evaluate the situation with a clearer, calmer and happier head.

But it goes deeper than that. For many of you, the techniques in this book will have given back to you a fresh, creative, fun and youthful outlook on life. It's so easy to become bogged down in serious matters – you've only got to look in newspapers or on TV to be swept up in the belief that the world is a negative and dangerous place. In our daily lives we are also too often bound by rules, regulations and fears which stifle change, diversity and positivity. Once you open up your mind to fun, and all the possibilities it brings, you will realise that life is in fact full of opportunity and laughter – that, in essence, is the power of Laughology.

# APPENDIX:
# FREQUENTLY ASKED QUESTIONS

## DO I HAVE TO BE FUNNY TO USE LAUGHOLOGY?

The simple answer to this question is no. Laughology is not about being funny or clowning around or continually joking about a situation. The Laughology model is about looking at life in a different way and lifting mood. Humour, as discussed throughout this book, is a way to process information from the outside world in order to feel differently about it internally, and thereby change our state of mind. As we grow up we learn to deal with information in many different ways; humour is one of these learnt processes. It gives us the power to intervene and make a change for the better.

## WHEN SHOULD I USE LAUGHOLOGY?

Laughology can be very personal and it is not always suitable to share your humour with others. In Chapter 5 we considered how humour and laughter are used in different situations and occupations and how occasionally they might be perceived as inappropriate if heard or used with others from outside that profession. However, in these contexts dark humour can help some individuals to cope with very difficult situations and move forward quickly, rather than becoming emotional about what they have experienced. It is hard to say whether using Laughology in this way is either wrong or right. The most important rule to remember is that it should be used as a positive tool to help you and others progress in a situation. It should never be used to belittle or to make others feel negative about themselves or their environment.

# ISN'T CRYING SOMETIMES GOOD FOR YOU?

Of course crying is good for you – it is a powerful emotional response, just like laughter. But it's all about balance. Crying and laughter are personal reactions to events and it is very important to express how you feel. If you want to cry about something that makes you feel sad (or even happy), this is a positive response. Emotional balance and resilience is the key to a happy and productive life. Laughology helps you to be resilient in difficult situations – such as at work or a challenging period in your life – when you want to feel more in control. Crying may be a part of the natural healing process at this time, but Laughology is about being able to pick yourself up and get through days when you feel you need a positive focus.

# DO SOME PEOPLE JUST NOT HAVE A SENSE OF HUMOUR?

A sense of humour and other people's perception of humour is very subjective. It depends on many things: how someone is brought up, the mood they are in, their line of work, what is happening in their lives at the time and many more factors. Just because an individual may come across (in your view) as gloomy, not up for a laugh, in a bad mood or negative, it doesn't mean they don't have a sense of humour. It may just be they have learnt to be this way, that their moods and feelings are demonstrated differently or they laugh and are happy in other situations.

# WHY DON'T PEOPLE LAUGH AT MY JOKES?

The whole ethos of Laughology is *your* attitude and how that makes you (and others) feel. If you think that telling jokes is a good way to get people on your side, you may well be wrong – especially if you're not very good at telling jokes! Ironically, in school I was renowned for not being able to tell jokes; however, what I did do well was being optimistic and happy. My jokes were terrible, but people liked my upbeat, fun and positive personality combined with a fair amount of self-deprecation. As a stand-up I found that jokes were not the 'in thing'; instead audiences liked real-life stories. Everyone enjoys a good anecdote – events from your life, mishaps and faux pas. We love it because it reminds us that we are all human and make mistakes. So, rather than having a list of one-liners, try to be truthful and talk about things that have happened to you – people are more likely to find true life funny and therefore are more likely to listen.

# WHY DO WE LAUGH WHEN SOMEONE FALLS OVER?

We look at life in terms of patterns and we pre-empt situations and their outcomes by calling on stored memories and experiences. We draw primarily on the part of the brain called the basal ganglia – the bit I like to describe as the brain's filing cabinet – where we store our accumulated knowledge. We tend to use this part of our brain to help us work through novel experiences, learning new from old. We are habitual creatures and like to look at the world in terms of how we expect it to be. If someone is walking alongside us our expectation is that he or she will continue walking or may overtake us or turn off in a different direction. Humour arises if the unexpected happens, so if that person falls over we might well laugh at the incongruity and unexpectedness of the situation. That is why shows like *You've Been Framed!* are so popular. We aren't amused by people's misfortunes; we are laughing at the shocking and unexpected. If we watch the same scenario repeatedly it loses its shock value and stops becoming funny.

The same theory works with jokes – they are funnier the first time you hear them. This explains why some comedians use progressively darker humour and increasingly shocking material as their career progresses. They have to maintain that shock value as they progress and sometimes they run the risk of being outrageous rather than funny. Once we start to expect the shocks they lose their impact and become less funny. Sacha Baron Cohen, the man behind the comedy creations Ali G and Borat, has displayed this progression. His early character Ali G was, in my opinion, laugh-out-loud funny because the humour he employed – showing other people's prejudices through the prism of the ignorance of his character – was fresh and unexpected. Baron Cohen's next incarnation, Borat, needed to be equally as funny and so was even more shocking than Ali G. The humour still worked. However, by the time he made his third comedy character, Brüno, the joke was wearing thin and the eponymous film set out to offend even more than *Borat*. However, because the audience was expecting the shocks I thought the jokes were less funny.

# BIBLIOGRAPHY

Armstrong, T. (1998). *Awakening Genius in the Classroom*. London: Atlantic Books.

Bernstein, D. A., Clarke-Stewart, A., Penner, L. A., Roy, E. J. and Wickens, C. D. (2000). *Psychology*, 5th edn. Boston, MA: Houghton Mifflin.

Bernstein, M. J., Sacco, D. F., Brown, C. M., Young, S. G. and Claypool, H. M. (2010). 'A preference for genuine smiles following social exclusion', *Journal of Experimental Social Psychology* 46: 196–199.

Brown, D. (1991). *Human Universals*. New York: McGraw-Hill.

Burton, S. (n.d.). 'Why not laugh?' Available at http://www.sburton.com/whynotlaugh.htm (accessed 31 May 2012).

Charlton, B. G. (2006). 'The rise of the boy-genius: psychological neoteny, science and modern life', *Medical Hypotheses* 67: 679–681.

Clifford, C. (1996). *Not Now … I'm Having a No Hair Day*. Minneapolis, MN: University of Minnesota Press.

Clifford, C. (2002). 'As simple as A, B, C' (February). Available at http://www.thebreastcaresite.com/tbcs/CommunitySupport/FunnyYouMentionItPage/AsSimpleAsABC.htm (accessed 31 May 2012).

Cousins, N. (1979). *Anatomy of an Illness as Perceived by the Patient: Reflections on Healing and Regeneration*. New York: Norton.

Darwin, C. (1872). *The Expressions of Emotions in Man and Animals*, 1st edn. London: John Murray.

Eagleman, D. (2011). *Incognito: The Secret Lives of the Brain*. New York: Pantheon/Random House.

Frankl, V. (2006). *Man's Search for Meaning*. Boston, MA: Beacon Press.

Freud, S. (1927) 'Der Humor', *Almanach* (1928): 9–16.

Freud, S. (1960[1905]), *Jokes and Their Relation to the Unconscious*, ed. and trans. by J. Strachey. In *The Standard Edition of the Complete Psychological Works of Sigmund Freud*, vol. 8. London: Hogarth Press/Institute of Psychoanalysis, pp. 8–236.

Fry, W. (1979). 'Mirth and the human cardiovascular system', in H. Mindess and J. Turek (eds), *The Study of Humor*. Los Angeles, CA: Antioch University Press, pp. 56–61.

Gross, J. J., Fredrickson, B. L. and Levenson, R. W. (1994). 'The psychophysiology of crying', *Psychophysiology* 31: 460–468.

Keltner, D. and Bonanno, G. A. (1997). 'A study of laughter and dissociation: the distinct correlates of laughter and smiling during bereavement', *Journal of Personality and Social Psychology* 73: 687–702.

LaFrance, M. (2011). *Lip Service: Smiles in Life, Death, Trust, Lies, Work, Memory, Sex, and Politics*. New York: W. W. Norton.

Martin, R. (2007). *The Psychology of Humor: An Integrative Approach*. Burlington, MA and San Diego, CA: Elsevier Academic Press.

Mobbs, D., Greicius, M. D., Abdel-Azim, E., Menon, V. and Reiss, A. L. (2003). 'Humor modulates the mesolimbic reward centers', *Neuron* 40: 1041–1048.

Provine, R. R. (2000). *Laughter: A Scientific Investigation*. New York: Viking Books.

Snowden Crosman, A. (2005). *Young at Heart: 61 Extraordinary Americans Tell How to Defy Age with Zest, Work and Healthy Lifestyles*, rev. edn. Bothell, WA: Book Publishers Network.

Sullins, E. S. (1991). 'Emotional contagion revisited: effects of social comparison and expressive style on mood convergence', *Personality and Social Psychology Bulletin* 17: 166–174.

Szabo, A. (2003). 'The acute effects of humor and exercise on mood and anxiety', *Journal of Leisure Research* 35(2): 152–162.

Tankersley, D., Stowe, C. J. and Huettel, S. A (2007). 'Altruism is associated with an increased neural response to agency', *Nature Neuroscience* 10: 150–151.

University of Maryland Medical Center (2005). 'University of Maryland School of Medicine study shows laughter helps blood vessels function better' (7 March). Press release available at http://www.umm.edu/news/releases/laughter2.htm (accessed 31 May 2012).

van Hooff, J. (1972). 'A comparative approach to the phylogeny of laughter and smiling', in R. A. Hinde (ed.), *Non-Verbal Communication*. Cambridge: Cambridge University Press, pp. 209–240.

Warren, J. E, Sauter, D. A, Eisner, F., Wiland, J., Dresner, M. A., Wise, J. S., Rosen, S. and Scott, S. K. (2006). 'Positive emotions preferentially engage an auditory–motor "mirror" system', *Journal of Neuroscience* 26: 13067–13075.

Watson, K. (2011). 'Gallows humor in medicine', *Hastings Center Report* 41(5): 37–45.

Wellcome Trust (2006). 'Laugh and the whole world laughs with you: why the brain just can't help itself' (13 December). Press release available at http://www.wellcome.ac.uk/News/Media-office/Press-releases/2006/WTX034939.htm/ (accessed 31 May 2012).

# INDEX

# NOTES

# NOTES

# NOTES

# NOTES

# NOTES

...............................................................
...............................................................
...............................................................
...............................................................
...............................................................
...............................................................
...............................................................
...............................................................
...............................................................
...............................................................
...............................................................
...............................................................
...............................................................
...............................................................
...............................................................
...............................................................
...............................................................
...............................................................

# NOTES

........................................................................

........................................................................

........................................................................

........................................................................

........................................................................

........................................................................

........................................................................

........................................................................

........................................................................

........................................................................

........................................................................

........................................................................

........................................................................

........................................................................

........................................................................

........................................................................

........................................................................

........................................................................

# NOTES

# NOTES

........................................................................
........................................................................
........................................................................
........................................................................
........................................................................
........................................................................
........................................................................
........................................................................
........................................................................
........................................................................
........................................................................
........................................................................
........................................................................
........................................................................
........................................................................
........................................................................
........................................................................
........................................................................
........................................................................
........................................................................

# NOTES

..............................................................................

..............................................................................

..............................................................................

..............................................................................

..............................................................................

..............................................................................

..............................................................................

..............................................................................

..............................................................................

..............................................................................

..............................................................................

..............................................................................

..............................................................................

..............................................................................

..............................................................................

..............................................................................

..............................................................................

# NOTES

# NOTES

..............................................................................
..............................................................................
..............................................................................
..............................................................................
..............................................................................
..............................................................................
..............................................................................
..............................................................................
..............................................................................
..............................................................................
..............................................................................
..............................................................................
..............................................................................
..............................................................................
..............................................................................
..............................................................................
..............................................................................
..............................................................................

The Laughology method helps with thinking skills, encourages positive engagement and organisational development. It promotes great leadership skills and enhances health and well-being.

As a company we deliver training to small and large organisations in the private and public sector in settings as diverse as schools, hospitals and multinational blue chip companies.

For general enquiries or to make a booking for any of our courses, workshops or consultancy services visit our website www.laughology.co.uk or contact:

Suite 869, Kemp House,
152–160 City Road,
London EC1V 2NX
T: 0844 800 1701
E: info@laughology.co.uk
www.laughology.co.uk